NATIONALITY QUESTION IN ASSAM
THE EPW 1980-81 DEBATE

NATIONALITY QUESTION IN ASSAM THE EPW 1980-81 DEBATE

Editor
Abu Nasar Saied Ahmed

OMEO KUMAR DAS INSTITUTE OF SOCIAL CHANGE AND DEVELOPMENT
Guwahati
&
AKANSHA PUBLISHING HOUSE
New Delhi-110 002 (India)

AKANSHA PUBLISHING HOUSE
4649-B/21, Ansari Road,
Darya Ganj,
New Delhi-2
Phone: 23263193,9811582579
E-mail: ektabooks@yahoo.com

Nationality Question in Assam : The EPW1980-81 Debate

First Published: 2006

ISBN .-81-8370-038-1

PRINTED IN INDIA

Published by M.P. Misra for Akansha Publishing House, New Delhi -110002 & Printed at Tarun Offset Printers Delhi

Dedicated

to

the memory of

Krishna Raj

a scholar-crusader for social justice

Contents

Abbreviations

AAGSP	: All Assam Gana Sangram Parishad
AAMSU	: All Assam Minority Students' Union
AASU	: All Assam Students' Union
AGP	: Asom Gana Parishad
AJD	: Assam Jatiyatabadi Dal, Asom Janata Dal
ALC Proc.	: Assam Legislative Council Proceedings
ASEB	: Assam State Electricity Board
ASS	: Asom Sahitya Sabha
ATPA	: Assam Tea Planters Association
BBC	: British Broadcasting Centre
BCP	: Bharatiya Chah Parishad
BJP	: Bharatiya Janata Party
CIA	: Central Intelligence Agency
CITU	: Centre of Indian Trade Unions
CPI (M)	: Communist Party of India (Marxist)
CPI (M-L)/ SNS	: Communist Party of India (Marxist-Leninists)/Satya Narayan Singh
CPI (M-L)	: Communist Party of India (Marxist-Leninists)
CPI	: Communist Party of India
CRP	: Central Reserve Police
DMK	: Dravida Munnetra Kazhagam

EPW	:	Economic and Political Weekly
FERA	:	Foreign Exchange Regulation Act
GNP	:	Gross National Product
GSP	:	Gana Sangram Parishad
HFC	:	Hindustan Fertilizer Corporation
HPC	:	Hindustan Paper Corporation
ICC	:	Indian Citizenship Certificates
IIT	:	Indian Institute of Technology
IMDT	:	Illegal Migrants (Determination by Tri-bunals) (Act)
INTUC	:	Indian National Trade Union Congress
IPTA	:	Indian People's Theatre Association
ITA	:	Indian Tea Association
JCI	:	Jute Corporation of India
MLA	:	Member of Legislative Assembly
MP	:	Member of Parliament
NaAGP	:	New AGP (Na Asom Gana Parishad)
NRC	:	National Register of Citizens
PDP	:	People's Democratic Party, Assam
PLP	:	Purbanchaliya Loka Parishad
PUCL	:	People's Union for Civil Liberties
RCPI	:	Revolutionary Communist Party of India (Rasik Bhatt)
RSPI	:	Revolutionary Socialist Party of India
RSS	:	Rashtriya Swayamsevak Sangha
SDO	:	Sub Divisional Officer
SFI	:	Students' Federation of India
SMS	:	Short Messaging Service
STATFED	:	Assam State Co-Operative Marketing and Consumers Federation Limited
SUCI	:	Socialist Unity Centre of India
TAI	:	Tea Association of India
USF	:	United Students' Federation
UGC	:	University Grants Commission

List of Contributors

Abu Nasar Saied Ahmed, Professor and Director, Omeo Kumar Das Institute of Social Change and Development, Guwahati, Assam

Amalendu Guha, Social Scientist and Retired Professor, Centre for Studies in Social Sciences, Kolkata

Gall Omvedt, Senior Fellow, Nehru Memorial Museum and Library, New Delhi

Hiren Gohain, Former Professor of English and Dean, Faculty of Arts, Gauhati University, Guwahati, Assam

Lily Bar a, Writer

Sanjib Baruah, Visiting Professor, Centre for Policy Research, New Delhi

Tilottama Misra, Professor, Department of English, Dibrugarh University, Assam

Udayon Misra, Professor, Department of English, Dibrugarh University, Assam

Introduction

The historic Assam movement has become a matter of the past. The euphoria, the emotion and the political contours of the movement disappeared with the formation of the Asam Gana Parishad led government soon after the historic election of 1985. But the intellectual debate that took place during the heyday of the movement did not die down. It remained in the scattered pages of academic journals and publications.

An unusually long movement involving various shades of people of the state, the Assam movement started in 1979 with an allegation that a large number of foreigners, more particularly the immigrant Muslims, and also the Bengali Hindus, got themselves enrolled in the voters' list of Mangaldoi Lok Sabha constituency of the state. The death of Hiralal Patowari, the sitting Member of Parliament from the constituency warranted the preparation for a by-election. As the preparation began, there was an allegation that the names of an alarming figure of 45,000 immigrants got entered in the revised voters' list. The All Assam Students' Union (AASU) started an agitation demanding the deletion of the immigrants' name from the voters' list and their deportation from the country. A newly constituted body named the All Assam Gana Sangram Parishad (AAGSP) joined the agitation making it a massive movement which continued for six years. While the movement leaders claimed that it was a peaceful Gandhian movement, others saw its violent and fascist character. It ended with the conclusion of the Assam Accord (See Appendix) in New Delhi between the Union Government of India and the movement leaders at the midnight of August 15, 1985. A new political party was formed by the movement leaders named the Asom Gana Parishad (AGP) in two months after the Accord. The key figures in the AASU and the AAGSP took rein of the new party. As a part of political dispensation and expediency associated with the provisions of the Accord, the State Assembly was dissolved in October and a fresh election was held in December. The newly formed AGP scored an emphatic victory and captured power in the state. The formation of the new Government at Dispur apparently sealed for good any prospect of reviving the movement, whether or not the main issue for which the movement was spearheaded would be addressed decisively in the near or distant future. It appeared that the only objective of the six year long Assam agitation against illegal migration was to capture power at Dispur by the movement leaders.

The movement period witnessed an unprecedented wave of academic exercises including publication of a large number of articles and books covering various aspects of the movement. These publications represent essentially two diametrically opposite views, one supporting the rationale, strategy and nature of the movement while the other attempted at exposing the intolerant and chauvinistic dimension of the movement imperilling the basic foundation of the composite society of Assam.

The *Economic and Political Weekly* (EPW) took the lead in publishing a number of epoch-making articles. These articles generated an intellectual debate on the nature, the content and the rationale of the Assam movement spearheaded by the AASU and the AAGSP. The publication of an article entitled "Cudgel of Chauvinism" in the *Economic and Political Weekly* (February 23, 1980, pp. 418-20) by Hiren Gohain was the starting point of the debate. It questioned the general impression created by the local and national press that the Assam movement was essentially a peaceful one and tried to demystify the British policy of importing people from outside the geographical boundaries of Assam. While expressing doubt on the rationality of the movement, Gohain finds a class character in the movement leadership. The ruling class received a jolt at the electoral success of the CPI (M) and other Left parties in the 1978 election. The CPI (M) alone captured 11 out of the 126 seats in the Assam Legislative Assembly and other Left constituents captured three seats. The chauvinists initiated attack on this 'Bengali' party, the CPI (M), and tried to turn the general discontentment of the local people against the Central Government and also against the emerging Leftist forces. The author makes a point to unmask the non-violent character of the movement by citing incidences of violence, which bred counter-violence from the state machinery. He concludes that chauvinism had been the 'deadly enemy' of all radical and democratic forces in the state, for which the process of integration of non-Assamese into the Assamese society has not been a success. A brief note entitled "Ganging-Up against the Left" which appeared in the *Economic and Political Weekly* (March 1, 1980, p. 465) testifies to the assertion of Hiren Gohain that the movement had a fascist character.

The article of Hiren Gohain provoked the publication of letters and articles in the journal depicting a genuinely human face of the movement, and rationalizing the socio-political and economic bases of the movement. Gail Omvedt not impressed by the assertion that Assam movement was directed against the Bengali speaking people, raised four questions in her letter to the Editor *of Economic and Political Weekly* (March 22, 1980, p. 580).

Although the article of Gohain initiated the debate on the nature, the character and the rationality of the Assam movement, the article of Amalendu Guha entitled "Little Nationalism turned Chauvinist: Assam's Anti-Foreigners Upsurge 1979-1980" in the *Economic and Political Weekly*

(Special Number, October 1980, pp. 1699-1720) became the central foci of the intellectual debate on the whole issue. It was responded to by leading figures of academia in Assam. The articles, comments and some letters relevant to the issue remained scattered in different volumes of the journal. There has been a growing demand among the younger generation, who did not witness the events of those historic years, to scan the views on the movement as such and to form their own opinion on it. This is quite a natural and welcome reaction of the younger generation, for the young researchers undertaking serious studies on socio-political dynamics in the state consider the Assam movement phase as a landmark in contemporary history of the state. Many new and significant dimensions have surfaced affecting and altering the societal contours of the state. The need to have these articles in a volume propelled us to think for the publication of all these articles in the form of a book in order to make them easily accessible to the readers.

As stated already, the debate on the rationale behind and the modus operandi of the Assam agitation against the illegal migrants to the state was steered by the publication of Guha's article. In his article Amalendu Guha, the author of a seminal work entitled *Planter- Raj to Swaraj: Freedom Struggle and Electoral Politics in Assam 1826-47* (New Delhi, 1977) states that he found inadequacy in understanding the logic and rationality of the Assam movement which had just begun with the reports that names of several thousand illegal migrants were entered in the electoral roll prepared for the bi-election to be conducted at the Mangaldoi constituency, which fell vacant at the death of the sitting Member of Parliament named Hiralal Patowari. The movement leaders presented a plea that the illegal migrants stood as a source of both potential as well as real danger to the survival of the Assamese as a nationality, for they feared that if the influx was not checked and was allowed to continue, the Assamese as a distinct community would be swamped away by the non-Assamese migrants. To Guha, the movement, undoubtedly, was related to the national question, which had the weakest link with the rest of Indian polity. In this article he looks beyond his period and analyzes the movement from a Marxian perspective and draws certain conclusions, which provoked significant response. He considers the putative concept of threat to the Assamese culture a myth than a reality. The theory that the Assamese society is in danger is a mechanization of the middle class Assamese who has instilled in the mind of the common masses a fear psychosis to whip up a spontaneous movement. Such an induced spontaneity of the masses based on unfounded fear turned the little Assamese nationalism to chauvinism. Thus, it became a middle class movement of a section of the great Assamese society against another section of greater Assamese society who were neither oppressor nor did they constitute a threat to the well-founded Assamese society. Spontaneity of the masses, as Lenin argued, unless guided by a disciplined and dedicated party, is always dangerous. The students, who constituted core of the movement, were not its originators. Their spontaneity was also induced by the upper class of the Assamese society who controlled the media and public opinion. Therefore, the ideological and organizational roots of the movement rested in this class of people. They planned and prepared meticulously the movement in 1978 and used the students as instruments for achieving the political objectives through the upsurge.

Dismissing the contentions of Gail Omvedt and Sanjib Baruah describing the Assam movement against the illegal migrants as peaceful, non-violent in essence and as a rebellion for self-expression, Guha argues that the Assam movement was national in form but chauvinist and undemocratic in manifestation. Therefore, its methods represented its intolerant and fascist face. It also presented a dubious character. It tried to show a non-violent and peaceful image when it tried to impress upon the rest of the country, but its dealing with the dissidents and minorities, both linguistic and religious, was coercive and hence violent. This had alienated the small nationalities in the state, which were likely to cause centrifugal tendencies in the composite nature of the Assamese society. History is full of such examples when little nationalism had bred chauvinism causing gravest harm to the society. In this way a movement launched towards self-determination eventually tends to become self-destructive.

Guha has put forward his arguments as to how healthy little nationalism professed by Anandaram Dhekiyal Phukan, Benudhar Rajkhowa and a few other icons of the Assamese society eventually turned into chauvinism and 'minority baiting' in character following the independence and partition of the country, on a false fear generated by the emergent middle class of being overwhelmed by the migrants. Little nationalism has an ideology of its own. It has its own symbols and heroes. If the Asamiya language acts as its unifying symbol, Lachit Borpukan symbolizes the national pride. These symbols were promoted in the colonial era as a part of the British strategy to divert the Asamiya elite from the Indian National Congress. But soon after independence, the attempt to impose the language on the unwilling minorities eventually proved to be self-defeating. Instead of making a larger space for the Asamiya nationalism to flourish, it circumscribed its wings. The unregulated chauvinism belittled the prospects of Asamiya little nationalism for natural growth and expansion. The blame for this retarded development undoubtedly goes to the Asamiya middle class.

The Asamiya middle class, having no space in the community of big bourgeoisie and their foreign collaborators, found the Bengali speaking community its competitor. Consequently, it geared up all its resources including the media to foment an upsurge of cutting the Bengali and other non-Assamese competitors to size. This had carried every potentiality of putting the assimilation process back to square. Certain constituent wings of the Asamiya middle class spearheaded the movement on the premises of hate nurtured in an atmosphere of economic stagnation and relative deprivation in which the state had been suffering for a considerable period.

An atmosphere of administrative chaos and lawlessness during the agitation period made it easy to ignite violence and genocide in the wake of the 1983 election. As Guha observes, it had been directed not only against the linguistic and religious minorities but also against the left parties -all of whom argued in favour of detection, disenfranchisement and deportation only after taking into consideration the due process of the national law and the international obligations. The movement leaders considered these procedures as stumbling blocks on the road to detect and deport the illegal immigrants coming from the neighbouring countries, more particularly from present Bangladesh.

While raising the definitional issues such as who is a foreigner, what is his class base and how fast their number is growing in absolute and relative terms, and what is their growth rate, Guha tries to dismiss the various contentions of Gail Omvedt and Sanjib Baruah. He disputes the proposal of Gail Omvedt to reduce the migrants substantially by uprooting them from the land where they had been living. Taking the lesson from history, Guha explains how the Nazis' plan to exterminate the Jews, Pakistan's proposal of exchanging its non-Muslims for India's Muslims, and the attempts of the Ahom king to exterminate the Mayamarias caused unmitigated disaster. Therefore, while rejecting the proposal of Omvedt, Guha finds substance and inherent values in the assimilation as testified to by such an example as that of the Ukranians with the Russians, an effort made by Lenin successfully. Ukraine, since the break-up of the Soviet Union, has a large population of Russian origin. Despite stresses and strains, the assimilation process still continues. Guha asserts that the process of assimilation takes quite a longer time. The Tai-Ahoms took three hundred years to assimilate with the local people. The process of assimilation of Bengali-speaking people with the Assamese had started. It was wrong to assume that the process was complete., just as it was wrong to argue that assimilation had not started or it was politically motivated or was fraught with a conspiracy angularity. Guha disabuses the apprehension of Sanjib Baruah that the Bengali Muslims one day would join hands with the Bengali Hindus to put the assimilation process back to square one. To him, the assimilation has an enduring economic basis, once the process starts, it should be promoted to ensure a larger Asamiya nationality.

Guha laments the way the chauvinists tried to disrupt the process of assimilation by launching into a long tirade against the Bengali speaking community of the Asamiya society. There were numerous instances of mass frenzy directed against them, a step not compatible with a practical solution to the problem of migration of foreign nationals into the state. He does not dispute the genuineness of the problem of migration nor does he undermine the argument that Assam should not be burdened with further influx. He suggests a twin strategy - border fencing which might bring the influx of Bangladeshi migrants to a standstill and assimilation of those who could not but be allowed to settle in places where they have already settled so that they too become an integral part of the greater Assamese society.

While agreeing to some of the assertions made by Tilottama Misra, i.e. that the extra-region and regional bourgeoisie and feudal interest groups have exploited resources in Assam, Guha observes that since the colonial era, Assam had been playing the role of supplying raw materials to the rest of the country. In this way Assam is being exploited by the national bourgeoisie. At the same time, he finds that there is no basis to argue that the toiling Bengalis, Nepalis and similar working people and peasants are the exploiters. The plight of this working population is in no way different from those living in other parts of the country. To him it is a fait accompli that the peasants and working class in Assam, as it is in the case of other states of India, are oppressed and exploited in an economic system in which extra-regional big business dominates the regional economy of the country. To do away with the regional disparity and exploitation, a strategy to whip up emotion against a particular class of people appears to be a misguided exercise.

The solution to the foreigner's issue in a multi-ethnic and composite society like that of Assam, Guha argues, lies essentially in the process of unhindered assimilation rather than deportation of the migrants who had already become an inseparable part of the Assamese society. The more practical approach to the problem of influx would be to seal the border with Bangladesh so as to zero down the rate of migration of the foreign nationals. The author finds only one positive element in the movement. The illusion that the common man had about the middle class leadership in the state began to fade out.

Guha's article invoked sharp reaction from Udayon Misra, Gail Omvedt and Sanjib Baruah. On the other hand, whereas Hiren Gohain finds merit in the basic premises of Amalendu Guha, Udayon Misra refutes the argument of Guha that Assamese little nationalism was responsible for the separation of Sylhet from Assam. Citing Guha's own contention, Misra argues that historically Sylhet was a part of Bengal and it was a colonial dispensation, which made it a part of Assam. While contesting the analysis of Guha on the demographic composition of the Assamese, Misra states that there had been rise in the Bengali speaking population to the tune of 41 per cent as against 31 per cent increase in the Assamese speaking population. Some other issues are sharply focused in Misra's critical response to Guha's article. To him and also to Sanjib Baruah, to paint a leading freedom fighter, Tarunram Phukan, as a chauvinist on the basis of an erroneous translation of his presidential address of the annual conference of the Asom Sahitya Sabha in 1927 is wrong. So are unacceptable the contentions that the immigrants being basically landless poor peasantry, their migration would not adversely affect the socio-religious balance of the demographic composition of the state and there could be assimilation of a highly developed Bengali culture with that of the Assamese,

Hiren Gohain finds little to contest Guha's 'sober and patient analysis' of the Assam movement. He considers that the 'morbid symptoms' of the Assam movement surfaced during 1972 when the AASU spearheaded a movement for the introduction of Assamese as the medium of instruction at the college level. While Guha finds certain values of "genuine democratic and national tendencies" in the language movement of 1972 and Sanjib Baruah tries to rationalize the Assamese middle class aspiration expressed in such movements, Gohain sees a fascist character in these developments. He considers that the Assamese outcry against immigration was a reflection of their frustration stemming out of their inability to check the influx of outsiders to the state of Assam. The left too was equally unsettled when it found it difficult to put the movement in the framework of economics. He, therefore, considers the Assam movement as a hangover from the colonial past.

Gail Omvedt takes space for addressing the issues she had raised on earlier occasions and to respond to the criticism launched by Guha in his seminal article. Replying to Guha's criticism of her contentions on the issue of self-determination, Omvedt argues that the right to self-determination of an oppressed nation could not be wished away only because of the fact that the oppressed nation had not demanded secession. Taking a similar line of argument as advanced by Udayon Misra and Sanjib Baruah, she also contests Guha's thesis of assimilation on the ground that the sign of assimilation shown by the Bengali Muslim was more political than real. More than two decades have passed since the culmination of the Assam movement with the signing of the Accord, the immigrant Bengali Muslims have become a part of the Assamese society. This irreversible process as it stands today may dispel the unfounded and induced apprehension of a section of the Assamese society that the decision of the Bengali Muslims to accept Assamese as the mother tongue needs to be viewed from a perspective broader than the narrowly framed political discourse. The 'material fear' of the Assamese people that they would be one day swayed away by the immigrants about whom Omvedt and others have articulated has not diminished over the years. That is why Omvedt finds a strong rational base of the Assam movement. Like Gohain, she also laments that the Left parties had failed to play a crucial role in the historic moment of the Assam movement.

Sanjib Baruah shares more or less a similar line of criticism spearheaded by Misra and Omvedt. While appreciating Guha's understanding of the Assam movement within the broader framework of the nationality question, Baruah advances a critique of Guha's stand that the Assam movement was an induced upsurge of chauvinism. He stands by his position in avoiding the use of the term 'self-determination' and his contention that there was genuineness in the fear of the Assamese nationality of being swamped by immigrants. The example of Tripura is too terrifying to be ignored. Like Guha, Baruah too do not consider the migrant Bengali community as an oppressor. But he does emphasize that the bitterness in the history of relations between the Assamese and the Bengalis on the language issue and the predominance of the Bengalis in the administration pointed out to the disturbing domination-subordination syndrome.

Over the years, since the end of the Assam movement, the tangled and troubled relationship between the two communities, the Assamese and the Bengalis, had died down. There is not a single instance of conflict and disturbance in the relationship. The old psyche of the dominant Assamese elite of being dominated by the Bengali community has never troubled the Assamese mind in the post-movement period. However, during the period of the movement there was a threat perception that the day was not too far when the Assamese would be overwhelmed by the surging immigrants. Sanjib Baruah tries to build his thesis that the threat perception is not without any valid foundation. One would find justification of the movement, if one takes into consideration the magnitude of the population pressure faced by the state. He feels that Guha's argument that the immigrants did not pose a threat to the

Assamese is ill founded, because the immigrants might change their stand on the language issue on political consideration. No one can dispel this apprehension since the immigrants' decision to identify themselves as Assamese is a political one. Baruah's long intervention includes issues like crisis in the dominant middle class, centre-state relations, problems of a multi-cultural society in Assam, faulty assimilation process involving the immigrant minorities and their aggressive hostility toward natives, fragility of the contention that the Assam movement is the product of foreign conspiracies, besides a clarification of the concept of plural society which he uses in his articles in the *Economic and Political Weekly* entitled "Cudgel of Chauvinism or Tangled Nationality Question" (March 15,1980, pp. 543-45) and "Beyond Patriots and Traitors" (May 17, 1980, pp. 876-78) which had invoked Guha's criticism. Finally, Baruah finds fault in the Left as it failed to examine critically the nationality question and cultural questions involved in it. The movement could not be easily dismissed as mere chauvinists' handiwork. It had deeper roots and one needs to examine all of them.

Sanjib Baruah's other article entitled "Beyond Patriots and Traitors" is a reply to Hiren Gohain's article "Tangled Theories". It is a reaffirmation of the arguments already set to roll that the Assam movement was reflective of the aspirations of the marginalized people.

The debate on the rationale of the Assam movement rests on the theory of exploitation of the rich resources of the state by the Union Government without at the same time creating a space for economic development of the state. One of the finest expressions of the theory is found in the article of Tilottama Misra, "Assam: Colonial Hinterland" (August 9, 1980, pp. 1353-64) which starts with an emphatic assertion that the Assam movement was rooted in the agitated mind of the people who had reasons to protest against the colonial exploitation of the resources of the state by the Indian state and the Indian capitalists. While highlighting the gravity of the exploitation, Misra finds genuineness of the popular anger at the Centre's apathy towards economic development of the state. The awareness of the people about the magnitude of exploitation, which was worse than in the colonial period, as she argues forcefully, had provided the rationale behind the popular upsurge. She has taken tea, mineral and other natural resource sectors as the areas of exploitation to prove her point that Assam had become a colonial hinterland. The exploitation and neglect were the twins, strong enough to steer a nation to spearhead a massive movement. Tilottama Misra deals with the other areas such as absence of infrastructure, industrial backwardness, inadequate power generation despite the existence of enormous power potentialities, poor transport facilities, discrimination against the local unemployed youth in the railway services to make it a point that while the central government in the post-colonial era had made Assam a colonial hinterland, it had done nothing to develop the state as well as the region. The people of Assam found a reasonably strong ground for spearheading a mass movement for economic and political self-determination, which could not be dismissed out rightly as parochial and chauvinist.

Amalendu Guha's response to the criticism of his article "Little Nationalism turned Chauvinists" appeared in the *Economic and Political Weekly* in two issues. He begins his reply taking up the criticism leveled against his article by Udayon Misra. All through the long reply, he maintains his position that the Assam agitation was an induced movement engineered by an internal and external class interest against those, who as a class had little capacity to pose a threat to the Assamese nationality. He stands by his conviction that the current process of progressive assimilation (as had been tried in Ukraine in the post-Bolshevik era) and not forced Asamiyaisation of all the immigrants should be encouraged. The ongoing assimilation process was not to be disrupted by the call of deportation of hundred thousands of already deeply rooted immigrants, as suggested by Sanjib Baruah and Gail Omvedt. He once again extensively deals with the Assamese nationality question in the context of problematic Indian national question and cites empirical evidences focussed on the magnitude of violence let loose by the chauvinists against those who did not fall on their line, besides of course against the linguistic and religious minorities. While replying to the observations made by Gail Omvedt on the role of the left in the movement, Guha deals with at length on the position of the left parties on various questions facing Assam, including the quest for tribal autonomy and the problems of oppressed people. He does not altogether dismiss the right of the oppressed people to struggle for self-determination. He argues that the Asamiyas were not the only oppressed people of the state. There were other small and oppressed groups too who needed space for development. Therefore, there was a need to examine the whole issue of self-determination of the oppressed people from a broader perspective than in a piecemeal manner. He continues to assert that the threat perception of the Assamese people, which appeared to have been central to the Assam agitation, is a myth. It is an induced fear, which had no foundation in the real sense of the term. He is of the firm opinion that in a multi-cultural society in which "ethnic factors are in a melting pot", economic development and political autonomy could stand as the basis for solution to many problems. To him, two other measures - encouragement to the process of assimilation and comprehensive measures to put to an end to influx - could be the only practical and acceptable steps to resolve the migration related crises in Assam.

An article by Lily Bara and a few letters to the editor have been reprinted here to present the concern of the readers on the Assam movement.

It is noteworthy that the Assam movement continued till the Assam Accord (Appendix) was signed at the mid-night of August 14, 1985. A number of historic and unprecedented events and incidents took place in Assam during the period 1979 to 1985. The Golap Borbora ministry fell on September 4, 1979 within 18 months of its formation as a result of factional crisis in the Janata Party, just like the fall of the Union Ministry headed by Moraraji Desai, which fell because of factional crisis and politically charged bargaining drama. Three ministries headed by three new faces were formed and were toppled in a successive row. They were - Jogen Hazarika who broke away from the Janata Party and formed Asom Janata Dal (September 9 to December 12, 1979), Syeda Anowara Taimur (December 6, 1980 to June 30, 1981) and Keshab Gogoi (January 13 to March 19, 1982). After the fall of the Gogoi ministry, the Assembly was dissolved. The Union Government took a position to hold the Assembly election in February to avoid a 'constitutional crisis'. The movement leaders and organizations opposed the election on the ground that no election could be considered legitimate until the voters' list was thoroughly revised to remove the entry of the names of doubtful migrants. Even in the teeth of strong and violent opposition, the 1983 election took place, which was marked by unprecedented violence and massacre, including the infamous Nellie massacre in a sleepy immigrant inhabitant village now in Marigaon district. The election installed Congress party to power headed by Hiteswar Saikia. He had to struggle hard against the onslaught of the opposition parties who had been raising the legitimacy question of the 1983 election. Despite his comfortable position in the Assembly, he had to submit to a political dispensation which demanded dissolution of the Assembly and a fresh mandate in the wake of the Assam Accord. The 1985 election took place in changed circumstances when everyone appeared to be in favour of it. The newly formed Asom Gana Parishad (AGP) captured power with a convincing majority and massive mandate in the Brahmaputra valley.

With the installation of the new AGP Government at Dispur, the principal cause, which remained central to the Assam movement, was forced to take the back seat in the political discourse and practice of Assam. The AGP rule earned notoriety for its mis-governance and misrule. The Government headed by Prafulla Kumar Mahanta was dismissed in

December 1990, the Assembly was dissolved and a fresh election was ordered. In the popular perception, the party that was formed with the blessings of the people of the Brahmaputra valley betrayed the people. Further, the AGP was split vertically. The splinter group formed a new party called the Na AGP (New AGP). The AGP was thrown out of power and the people brought back the Congress party to power once again in 1991, Though people gave another chance to the AGP in 1996, there was hardly any positive change in its style of governance. The scepter of 'secret killing' loomed large. There was economic stagnation with the fall in the gross national product (GNP) and per capita income. The scandalous relationship between the Chief Minister and an employee in the Assembly secretariat rocked the ruling party. The obvious result was the AGP was once again thrown out of power in 2001. The symptoms of AGP's fall was quite visible in the two parliamentary elections in 1998 and 1999 when it failed to capture a single seat. In 2004 Lok Sabha elections it has managed to capture two seats. Against the backdrop of its overall miserable performance as a party protecting and promoting Assamese nationalism, the AGP has faced yet another split. Its founder president Prafulla Kumar Mahanta was expelled from the party on July 4, 2005 for his alleged anti-party activities culminating the simmering cold war between him and the present president Brindaban Goswami. Mahantahas floated a new party named Asom Gana Parishad (Progressive). The factional rivalry and the intra-party conflict has therefore caused irreparable damage to the party that came into being with the pledge to serve the cause of Assamese nationalism. In this way, a party grown out of the six year Assam movement has gradually lost space in the imagination of the Assamese psyche as a saviour of regional interest.

It is noteworthy that Amalendu Guha advances that the immigrants had not been a threat to the Assamese society. Doubts had been expressed at that time on the efficacy of the threat thesis. A quarter of a century has passed. The immigrant community has fully integrated into the

Assamese society. Not only have they returned Assamese as the mother tongue at the time of census, they have been actively associating themselves with the cultural and literary life of Assam. The special session of the Asom Sahitya Sabha was held in an immigrant-dominated place called Kalgachia in 2002 with grandeur and enthusiasm making their commitment to the language and literature visible.

There has been objective assessment of the Assam movement in the recent years. The local media often publishes leading articles reviewing the movement. The reappraisals concentrate on highlighting the adverse effect of one-year academic loss during the movement period, the ethnic assertion of small and marginalized communities living in the state raising the question of their self-determination in an Assamese dominated power structure, and the problems of assimilation of immigrants. It is worthwhile to mention the edited volume of Hiren Gohain and Dilip Bora, *Asom Andolan: Pratisruti aru Falasruti* (a collection of articles in Assamese entitled Assam Movement: Promises and Results) which is an eye opener. The articles have tried to recapture the events and consequences of the movement from a realistic perspective and have found that except making the people aware of the magnitude of neglect perpetuated by the successive governments in New Delhi since independence, and the degree of exploitation of the natural resources of Assam for which the state has a case to be placed in the corridor of power at the centre, the movement has virtually done nothing but has harmed the interests of the people.

Although the foreign national issue appeared to have died down soon after the Assam Accord, it again surfaced recently after a period of two decades. It was kept alive within the gamut of Illegal Migrants Detection Tribunal (Act) [IMDT], which now stands nullified by the Supreme Court after the historic verdict on July 12, 2005. The Act was enacted in 1983 ostensibly to protect the indigenous Muslims from harassment caused by certain quarters. There were instances of harassment on indigenous Muslims when they were asked to prove themselves as Indian citizens. In the name of protecting the indigenous Muslims against such harassment, it is alleged, the Act ultimately protects the illegal migrants. While the AGP, the Bharatiya Janata Party and some others had been demanding that the IMDT should be replaced on the ground that it is discriminatory arrangement and thus it was injurious to the national interest, the Congress was in favour of retaining it so that no Indian citizen was unnecessarily harassed. It is interesting to note that despite the pronounced position taken by the AGP and the BJP to repeal it, the IMDT remained untouched, even though AGP ruled the state twice and the BJP was at the Centre for six years. At any rate, the issue of foreign nationals always appears in the political scene in Assam at the time of the state as well as national elections.

The issue of illegal migration remains a transitional political and electioneering issue to be forgotten soon after the elections. As the Assembly election due in 2006 is approaching, the issue once again returned to the political scene when an organization called Chiring Chapari Yuva Manch in Dibrugarh town of Upper Assam spearheaded a campaign against the 'Bangladeshi' national flocking into the town in the recent times. The Manch appealed to the people to take recourse to economic boycott of the people and sent SMS messages to the effect that no one should engage the 'Bangladeshi' nationals in any activity and give any scope for their livelihood. The campaign led to the exodus of several hundred 'Bangladeshi' people from Dibrugarh and later on from other parts of upper Assam. While some hailed this step uprooting the foreign nationals, others decried it as a handiwork of the communal forces to disturb peace in the state. The Government position is that these people are inter-district migrants, who hail from lower Assam and went to Dibrugarh and other places of upper Assam in search of livelihood. At any rate, the memories of the Assam movement years once again got reflected in the recent past, indicating thereby that political forces are active to reap in a big way by thereby that political forces are active to reap in a big way by raising this perennial and contentious issue from time to time.

Looking back it is not difficult to find that although the Assam movement apparently tried to address the nationality question in Assam while trying to protect and promote the aspirations of the Assamese speaking population living in the Brahmaputra valley, it was actually designed by the middle class Assamese elite as a strategy to capture the state power. The people of the valley enthusiastically voted them to power twice in two decades to be disillusioned totally. The electoral performance of the AGP indicates how fragile its support base is in the state. Soon after it was voted to power for the second time in 1996, the party saw the wrath of the people at the time of Lok Sabha polls in 1998 and 1999 when it drew a blank. The percentage of votes polled by the AGP in these two Lok Sabha elections was 12.7 and 11.9 respectively. Although it was routed in the Assembly elections of 2001 as well, it nevertheless improved its support strength to 20.02 per cent. Notwithstanding that it managed to capture only two out of 14 seats in the 2004 Lok Sabha poll, and thus tried to restore some credibility, a vertically divided political platform can hardly promote the cause for which it has been created. Therefore, the political scenario foretells that the Assamese nationality question has been relegated to sideline making regionalism a less important issue. Now it remains in the agenda of a section of the militants whose credibility and support base suffer from inherent impairment and contradictions. This makes the ground political situation easier for national political parties like the BJP and the Congress to consolidate their position among the electorate and eventually cause erosion of the stronghold of the undivided AGP. In the next election, battle line will be drawn between two national parties - the BJP and the Congress leaving hardly any room for regional sentiments to reemerge within a foreseeable time.

Late Krishna Raj gave adequate space in the *Economic and Political Weekly* to bring to the academic world the discourse on the Assam movement. But for his generous stand, the massive movement could have hardly reached the academic community. He permitted me to reprint the relevant articles in this edited volume. This volume has been dedicated to the fondling memory of Krishna Raj who passed away in 2004.

I am indebted to the authors who have allowed me to reprint their articles in this volume. My colleagues Anuradha Dutta, Partho Ghosb, Indranee Dutta, Bhupen Sarmah, Kalyan Das, Saswati Choudhury and Joydeep Baruah extended me their helping hand. I had a long discussion with Akhil Ranjan Dutta, a young and promising scholar and teacher at Gauhati University, on the need to put together all the relevant articles in an edited volume. His suggestions have been quite useful. Ratna Bhuyan, a Research Associate at the Institute, has helped me in doing the copy editing of the volume. I am grateful to all of them. Rustam Ali did the computer work efficiently. He deserves thanks. Besides doing the difficult task of proof reading, my wife Ruby has been a constant source of inspiration and it is her tireless encouragement that has made me compile and edit the work within a desired time frame. She too deserves my sincere thanks. Our efforts to bring out the great *Economic and Political Weekly* debates in one edited volume will not go in vain if it reaches the contemporary readers.

1

Cudgel of Chauvinism

—Hiren Gohain

It is the function of social science to penetrate the fog of ideology and discern the true shape and sequence of events. The recent disturbances in Assam have once again brought home this lesson to us. The agitation over the presence of so-called 'foreign nationals' has grown into a massive movement, bringing out into the streets hundreds of thousands of ordinary men and women passionately committed to defending Assam from an alleged 'silent invasion' by foreigners, sowing seeds of deep suspicion and mistrust among different communities who have been living as peaceable neighbours for generations, and causing outbreaks of mob violence in which hundreds have lost their lives and thousands have been uprooted from their homes.

In wide areas of northern Kamrup, a populous district, for about a week (January 4 to 10) mobs roamed from village to village, indulging in arson and massacring pitilessly helpless people, unmoved by wails of terrified women and children. The army had to be called in to establish some semblance of law and order and restrain the unruly mobs.

---

* *EPW,* Vol. XV, No. 8, February 23, 1980, pp. 418-20.

Yet national leaders of the stature of Atal Bihari Vajpayee have, according to press reports, found the movement "on the whole peaceful and democratic". M V Kamath, editor of *The Illustrated Weekly of India,* has written an article called "Neglected Assam" in his magazine where a similar view has been propounded with some show of factuality. It goes without saying that the press in Assam, with one or two exceptions has been painstakingly preparing just such a picture for local and outside consumption. They blacked out sporadic acts of violence, obscured or confused the circumstances in which these took place, and camouflaged the panic and terror among the threatened minority communities as peaceful support to the agitation. Even now it is engaged in covering the terrible atrocities in north Kamrup with phoney stories about the 'region of terror' created by the army and the CRP.

Few journalists and leaders have visited the affected areas, talked to inmates of the refugee camps or had discussions with spokesmen of the minority communities. It is obvious that they represent a kind of 'rotten compromise' between the all-India ruling class and the Assamese ruling elite, involving connivance at monstrous barbarities and breathtaking mendacity.

There is no denying the fact that over the last few decades there has been an unusual spurt of population growth in Assam, far outstripping the all-India rate of growth. That a good deal of this is due to the continuous immigration from Bangladesh (at one time Pakistan) and Nepal is beyond dispute. But it is yet to be ascertained how much of the growth is due to natural fertility and fall of the death rate, especially among the immigrant Muslims who had come before partition and Independence.

Immigration had been officially encouraged by the British who were anxious to put to some use vast stretches of virgin land in Assam. The Muslim League ministry in the forties tried to increase the population of Muslim voters in Assam by encouraging large-scale colonisation by poor

Muslim peasants in government reserve lands. Even after Independence, successive Congress ministries tried to contain the progress of Leftist forces by injecting constituencies with heavy doses of Muslim voters, usually smuggled from across the border.

Apart from lakhs of tea-garden labourers brought by the British tea-planters, the Assamese gentry too have been in the habit of bringing hardy Muslim peasants from across the border to turn thousands of acres of fallow land into smiling and luxuriant fields of jute and paddy. (The independent Assamese peasants were not interested in producing for the market or in intensive cultivation to that extent.)

Besides, in the decades before and after Independence, a steady stream of 'outsiders' from the rest of the country have been coming to meet the growing need for various kinds of skilled labour and professionals. Barbers, cobblers, mechanics, technicians, carpenters, blacksmiths and petty traders from 'outside' have been playing their trades without serious conflict with the indigenous people for generations.

Since the thirties, there have been instances of Assamese resentment and frustration at the progress of such cultivators, mechanics and petty traders. Petitions were sent to the Indian National Congress but were ignored by the national leaders. Besides, the tempo of the Independence movement helped sink such petty differences. But the fears remained. There was, further, the memory of the early years of British rule when the colonial authorities tried to suppress Assamese and replace it with Bengali as the official language.

In the decades after Independence 'the law of uneven development of capitalism' prevailed to the detriment of Assam which remained a backward' and underdeveloped state. Neither agricultural development nor industrialization kept pace with the needs of the growing population. Since the sixties unemployment has been acute. Seventy seven per cent of the local peasantry found themselves either completely landless or owners of uneconomic holdings. Since planning and development all over the country have been largely in the interest of monopoly capital, there has been no attempt to establish major industries to the point of burning up every year large quantities of natural gas.

The situation has thus become explosive. Popular discontent and indignation against 'the Centre' have simmered long enough and class organisations and class politics have become more and more familiar. The local ruling elite and their all-India senior partners got a rude jolt when in the last assembly elections the CPI (M) with a fledgling organisation bagged 11 seats. An important factor in the success of the CPI (M) was the fact that the erstwhile immigrants, now settled for decades and bearing the brunt of the widespread pauperization, no longer voted Congress in a pack, but sometimes voted for the CPI (M) and the Left parties.

Naturally, the ruling class started the counter-attack with the only effective weapon available to it - chauvinism. During the last assembly elections itself, there was propaganda launched by the Assam Jatiyatabadi Dal against the CPI (M) as a 'Bengali' party or as an instrument of 'Bengali expansionism'. The experiment paid off with the defeat of the strong CPI CM) candidate in Guwahati. As the background of the present movement one can unhesitatingly point to the year-long propaganda in the Assam press - skilfully mixing up news about influx of outsiders with stories of Bengali trickery, deceit and treachery. Most of the lurid crimes were reported to have been the work of such outsiders, and spectacular claims, mostly unfounded, were made about the extent and degree of foreign infiltration.

The press campaign began from about a year before the scheduled date of the parliamentary election. It was aided by a highly efficient machinery for spreading rumours and hearsay, so that inflated and colourful details of any supposed incident could travel by word of mouth for miles within a matter of minutes. There were articles, letters to the editor, and editorials in hundreds, accusing the Left parties and intellectuals of callousness to and betrayal of the fate of Assam. Rejoinders and rebuttals from the besieged leftists were either suppressed or given short shrift. News stories and careful management of the correspondence columns very soon created an atmosphere of terror and intimidation. Members of the minority communities were also forced to sign pledges and letters to the editor expressing total support to the cause of expelling 'foreigners'.

The anxiety and terror of the minority communities were aggravated by the deliberate confusion about the exact number of foreigners to be detected and expelled from Assam. Often the figures given in public meetings and the press were as high as five million or seven million, naturally making every non-Assamese feel that he would be on the list of such aliens, however just and strong his claim might be.

In the meantime, two prestigious organisations became involved in the movement. The Assam Sahitya Sabha, a 'non-political' body looking after the 'cultural interests' of Assam and the Assamese joined the leadership of the movement, so far in the hands of regional groups like Purbanchaliya Loka Parishad (PLP) and Assam Jatiyatabadi Dal (AJD). Secondly, the All Assam Students Union (AASU), a professedly non-political (meaning non-Left, and sometimes anti-Left) students organisation covering all the schools and colleges in Assam under flexible constitution, began to play a leading part.

The phase of statements, letters and public meetings was followed by a more militant and active phase of Satyagraha and picketing. Soon the middle class was deeply involved. By the middle of November, massive popular participation began to be noticed in the towns. The leadership was in the hands of a loosely organised 'Gana Sangram Parishad' with representatives from different, political and non-political bodies, though the most effective element in it was unquestionably the All-Assam Students' Union. The left parties were first isolated by a clever maneuver, and then made the target of vicious propaganda. Among the national parties too, one could see elements of Janata party (like Ajit Sarma, MP) and the Congress joining the agitation with unbridled enthusiasm.

A facade of non-violence and 'democracy' notwithstanding the atmosphere was fast deteriorating in November. The 'law and order' situation became extremely unpredictable with the Assam Police and the state administration lending unconcealed support to the movement. The Marwari traders joined in a body and helped to fan the flicker of anti-Left sentiment into a blaze. Violence erupted in eastern Assam towns like Tinsukia and Dibrugarh, where the Bengali minority came under attack. A section of the Bengali population, inspired by their brand of chauvinism, tried in some places to retaliate. The death of a bank officer was the first clear case of violence in the course of the movement to be reported. But the press lost no time in covering up the traces and blaming it on 'anti-social elements' and saboteurs. At this juncture, the RSS elements in the movement tried to divert the tension into anti-Muslim channels and nearly succeeded. The RSS General Secretary, Hajendra Singh, visited Assam and declared that the Hindus from Bangladesh should be allowed to stay on but the Muslims be driven out.

Since the youths in the movement were not given clear instructions as to the procedure for detection and expulsion of foreigners, since there was no strict discipline and control at the local level, and since extremists among the regional groups made a habit of coercive fascist practices, incidents of violence and intimidation were bound to increase. Many thought that the movement was committed to harrying the foreigners out of the 'sacred soil' of Assam. In north Guwahati students participated in a police attack on indigenous tribal peasants falsely given out as 'Bangladeshis'. A river-boat carrying 'Bangladeshis' to the paper-mill at Jogighopa was seized and two helpless members of the Muslim crew were butchered near Soalkuchi on November 10.

The spate of violence was triggered off by the death of an Assamese student leader at Bhawanipur in Kamrup district. The caretaker government at the Centre did little to meet the demands of the movement. By an extraordinary fluke the Janata government at the state capital had fallen some time ago and the new Chief Minister led a ramshackle ministry and feared collapse every day. This situation certainly encouraged the irresponsible elements and tendencies in the movement. The PLP had come out with a demand that the electoral rolls must be corrected before the elections took place. In many places farces of such 'correction' took place, deleting at a stroke hundreds of names of genuine voters, adding to the confusion. Soon the cry was taken up by the other groups and it was decided to prevent by force the submission of nomination papers by candidates announced by the all-India parties. Such candidates were *gheraoed* in their house. The Central Government did nothing stronger than announce that candidates wishing to submit nomination papers would be given police protection. Abida Ahmed, widow of the late President, was rescued from such a *gherao* by a convoy of armed police and CEP, which proceeded towards Barpeta. Volunteers of the movement offered resistance at several places on the way and were brutally beaten up by the CRP. In such a confrontation, a student leader lost his life near Barpeta on December 10, and at once he was acclaimed as the martyr of the movement. There was widespread indignation and grief throughout the state, fanned by a press on the alert.

This was the long-awaited trigger that sparked off a series of incidents where members of the leftist organisations and minority communities came under remorseless and brutal attack. Members of the CPI (M) and the SFI were carefully marked out and either killed, injured or kept on the run. Many are yet to return to their homes. Quite a few have been subjected to the public indignity of a forced recantation of Marxism. We have already indicated at the beginning the enormous extent and ferocity of violence in northern Kamrup. There is no doubt about popular involvement in such cases of destructive violence. There was also a certain degree of planning and co-ordination - as in simultaneous attacks in several places, wrecking of bridges and building of road blocks and use of motorized transport to carry mobs from place to place. It is enough to indicate the fury of the mob that on January 6 in a place near Mukalmua in northern Kamrup, a hamlet of sixty houses was entirely wiped out and even women and children were not spared.

In our opinion, such acts were not the result solely of conspiracy by isolated groups of saboteurs or provocateurs. There was popular enthusiasm for and participation in such ghastly acts. But such terrible enthusiasm had been generated by months of inflammatory propaganda in the press. Even the Guwahati centre of All-India Radio added to the intoxication by broadcasting burning patriotic songs and plays-even a talk on Human Rights was turned into a vindication of the rights of the 'neglected Assamese'! Political elements like the RSS also cannot disclaim their responsibility and may even have provided the element of discipline and organisation in these man hunts and massacres. Any impartial review of the press in Assam for the last six months would prove that the contagion of violence and inhumanity was largely spread by the press.

Chauvinism has since Independence been the deadly enemy of all radical and genuinely democratic forces in Assam. The Assamese ruling elite lack both the economic resources and cultural strength to be able to integrate non-Assamese groups into Assamese society. Yet it has not abandoned its dream of national resurgence in a capitalist set up. Hence it uses from time to time the cudgel of chauvinism to beat into submission non-Assamese groups who might resist the domination. Chauvinism is by nature authoritarian and fascist, and an ally of the Indian ruling class as a whole. This is the reason why eminent Indian intellectuals from outside the state have blessed the movement which has been a nightmare to thousands of innocent people. While the tyranny browbeats the non-Assamese working class and inspires the Assamese peasantry with dreams of refurbished 'national' glory, it receives support from Indian big traders and - yes, international capital.

2

Ganging-Up Against the Left

—Anonymous

During their fact-finding visits to Assam last month neither Atal Bihari Vajpayee and Ravindra Verma of the Janata party, nor Yashpal Kapoor and S D Sharma of the Congress (I) found any evidence of violence in current agitation on the 'foreign nationals' issue, being jointly led by the All Assam Gana Sangram Parishad and All Assam Students Union. If indeed there were some violent incidents, Congress (I) leaders alleged, they were all the doings of the CPI (M) and the RSS. As for the CPI (M) and its student organization, the SFI, the plain fact is that these parties and groups have refused to join the chauvinist band - wagon and consequently have been the victims of violence perpetuated against them by the chauvinists; and yet the Congress leaders from Delhi have accused them of being involved in the violent incidents! Here are some facts, widely known in Assam, though not equally widely reported in the local press.

On December 3, 1979, the CPI (M) office at Sorbhog was ransacked by members of the Chatra Sanstha and three party members were seriously injured in the attack. They

* *EPW,* Vol. XV, No. 9, March 1,1980, p. 465.

were hospitalized for almost seven weeks, being released on January 25. The party office at Barpeta Road too was attacked. At Bamiakuchi near Sarthebari, CPI (M) members and sympathizers were attacked by a bus-load of 'patriots' with the assistance of the police, taken to the Thana, and severely beaten. Other places where CPI (M) members and sympathizers have been attacked include Nalbari, Bambhay, Sootea, Tihu, Pathsala, Bhabanipur and of course Barpeta. A new feature of these attacks - new in Assam, that is - has been that many CPI (M) members and sympathizers have had to leave their homes and seek shelter elsewhere. The Assamese 'patriots' have in this respect overcome their traditional antipathy to the Bengalis and have adopted, wholesale, the tactics of Congressmen in West Bengal following the overthrow of the United Front government.

The most serious consequence of these incidents - apart from the fact that legitimate political activities by parties not supporting the present agitation are now virtually impossible - has been the free hand given to the armed forces to restore law and order in large areas on the north bank of the Brahmaputra where between January 4 and 8, the chauvinists reigned supreme, and where since January 7 when the Government of Assam declared the entire northern part of the Kamrup district comprising Barpeta and Nalbari sub-divisions and north Guwahati and Kamalpur police station areas as 'disturbed areas' and transferred the responsibility to maintain law and order to the army, the armed forces have reigned supreme. Several places in these areas are still under curfew. Before the armed forces took over, more than 12,000 persons (Bengali Hindus and Muslims as well as Assamese, the latter in Barpeta sub-division) had taken shelter in relief camps. After the army moved in, under the guise of protecting the minorities, the forces of law and order have been on a rampage and many reports have appeared in the local press of atrocities against the civilian population, particularly of molestation and rape. None knows exactly how many have died. Several hundreds, probably. While the killing of one Assamese student has been widely reported, the number of Bengalis killed is anybody's guess. Some idea of the number of dead may be had when complete normalcy is restored and those who have fled their homes come back.

The violence, killing and arson that preceded the entry of the army in north Kanirup was certainly pre-planned. Leaders from Guwahati held meetings in the area 'alerting' the local people of possible 'attack' from the minority communities, both linguistic and religious. Suddenly, it was announced over the loudspeaker that the attack had actually begun and trained hands began to kill and set fire to the house of 'foreign nationals' whose forefathers had migrated from East Bengal. The violence continued for four days, unchecked. Indeed, it is alleged that it was connived at by the state's bureaucracy; the deputy commissioner of Kamrup was at Nalbari during all these days to 'cover' his non-Assamese SDO. In Barpeta sub-division, one additional deputy commissioner, known to be sympathetic to the agitators, was posted to 'cover' the local SDO who also happened to be non-Assamese.

The culprits did their job and moved away before the police arrived. Now collective fine has been imposed on the neighbourhood.

3

Assam Cudgel of Chauvinism or Tangled Nationality Question?

—Sanjib Baruah

Hiren Gohain's characterization of the recent events of Assam *(EPW,* February 23) as chauvinism is not a novel one. Much of the national press, notably *The Statesman,* has been saying precisely that ever since the movement in Assam on the foreigners issue started nearly six months ago. It was a theme in the campaign speeches of Congress (I) leaders, though since the election one has heard much less of it. Whether there has been a radical shift in the attitude of those in power at the centre is still premature to say since two major incidents of CRP atrocities - one on peaceful demonstrators and the other while responding to a breakdown of law and order -have occurred since the change of government at the centre. If indeed there has been a change of attitudes on the part of ruling elites and sections of the national press the motivation for it may not be a conspiracy suddenly hatched up against the left - as Gohain believes. It may simply be because unlike Gohain, many other people are seeing the intensity of popular

* *EPW,* Vol. XV, No. 11, March 15,1980, pp. 543-45.

feelings in Assam on the issue in spite of the simultaneous occurrence of brutal incidents of violence. I fully share Gohain's concern over the monstrous violence that has taken place in Assam. But I do not think that it is necessary to deny the peacefulness of satyagrahas where thousands have participated and to label authentic reports of CRP violence "phoney" in order to draw attention to the incidents of violence primarily against the Hindu Bengali and Muslim Bengali communities, but also against the Assamese community and to the attacks on the left. Gohain begins his report by promising to "penetrate the fog of ideology" through dispassionate social science analysis. A social scientist, however, cannot afford to get carried away by the occurrence of violence that has a clear socio-political content. He has to measure precisely the extent and nature of that violence in relation to larger events and get to the roots of that social phenomenon rather than resort to explanations in terms of "mob fury" and "disturbances" - terms that rightly belong to the vocabulary of the gendarme.

Gohain's analysis of the events is a simple conspiracy theory. The left in Assam was getting strong; the evidence: the CPI (M) bagged eleven seats in the Assembly elections of 1977. The ruling classes trembled at the revolution of eleven Assembly seats and conspired to fight back with the 'cudgel of chauvinism". The highly manipultable Assamese masses of course in unison became pawns in this ruling class conspiracy. Running through Gohain's analysis is a single consideration - that the CPI (M) and SFI are under attack in Assam. Such attacks should of course be exposed and resisted. But how far do the attacks reflect the dominant character of the movement in Assam is debatable. The attacks on communists in the 1940s in the thick of the Quit India Movement, no matter how reprehensible in themselves, would not warrant the interpretation that anti-leftism was the primary content of Gandhi's movement. An aspect of the events in Assam like the attack on leftists cannot be seen in isolation from the whole set of events and from the chronology of how the attacks on leftists have come about. Why was the CPI (M) alone isolated for attack? Is it because of its influence? Or could it be that a number of statements made by Jyoti Basu - no matter how reasonable they seem if cited without reference to the particular group psychology that exists in Assam today - managed to alienate completely the CPI (M) from the Assamese people? A February 9 report in the *Mainstream* notes that unlike the CPI (M), the CPI was "not physically attacked until very recently", though along with "almost every political party" its credibility had eroded. A recent report of an attack on CPI involved an attempted eviction of tenants by landowners. To anyone familiar with the thousands of instances where landlords all over the country have evicted tenants following land reforms legislations, an attempt to exploit a movement demanding the expulsion of foreigners, the bulk of whom are peasants, is hardly surprising. Such attacks of course should not be condoned. But they cannot constitute the defining element of the complex events in Assam.

Hiren Gohain builds up his conspiracy theory with the help of a few more inaccuracies and half-truths, displaying skills no less than that of the Assamese press, which he rightly condemns, (a) He claims that "elements" of the Janata party and the Congress had joined the agitation with "unbridled enthusiasm". In support he cites the name of one Janata MP and not a single Congress personality! (b) He has quoted the RSS General Secretary Rajendra Singh's statement that Hindus from Bangladesh should be allowed to stay, but the Muslims sent back. He leaves out the important fact that all the organizations involved in the agitation in Assam have publicly condemned the statement, (c) According to Gohain, "since the youths in the movement are not given clear instructions as to the procedure for detection and expulsion of foreigners...... incidents of violence and intimidation were bound to increase". He cleverly implies that the leadership of the movement is calling for the expulsion of foreigners through mass action. That is blatantly untrue. The leadership, some may argue, is at least indirectly responsible for creating a climate of intimidation between various communities. But this type of reasoning, which overlooks the history of years of continued influx and indifference on the part of appropriate governmental authorities and the fact that the issue has now become the rallying point of a mass movement, befits the law and order bureaucrat and not the analyst of social movements, (d) The candidates of all India parties according to Gohain, were prevented by force from filling nomination papers in the last election. The truth is that the postponement of election was the major issue of the movement in Assam. Many candidates of regional as well as all India parties chose not to file nominations perceiving the popularity of the demand. Democratic elections are about popular support. When *gheraos* of candidates adamant on filing nominations involved tens of thousands of satyagrahis, it obviously did not make sense to most candidates to file nominations with the help of military and CRP convoys. (e) The Assam government and the Assam Police, according to Gohain, have given "unconcealed support" to the movement. In truth it was the state government employees' associations of all levels whose support for the demands of the movement has determined the incapacity of the state government to use its machinery to suppress the movement, as Gohain might have wanted, (f) Gohain only grudgingly grants the importance of the major issue of the movement -the influx of people from East Pakistan, and that too, when it suits his argument. According to him they were brought in by successive Congress governments trying to "contain the progress of Leftist forces". It is a far-fetched explanation for a phenomenon that started at the beginning of the century and is primarily rooted in economics, though the era of vote banks was certainly a contributory factor.

The problem with Gohain's analysis is that he refuses to take the question of influx into Assam, which rightly or wrongly is the central focus of the present events in Assam, seriously. It is not a question of agreeing or disagreeing with the aims of the Assam movement. But the fact is that immigration into Assam on a scale that has few parallels anywhere in the world, within a relatively short period of time, has hopelessly tangled Assam's nationality question.

In that single fact and the unwillingness of some leftists

to come to grips with that reality lies an explanation for why "chauvinism", as Gohain puts it, "has since Independence been the deadly enemy of all radical and genuinely democratic forces in Assam". The influx into Assam has a long history. The issue has been a central theme in Assam's politics at least since the 1930s, though since Independence it has been addressed more in the back rooms of political intrigues rather than as a public issue. It is false to expect to have an understanding of the events if one begins that history at 1977 when the CPI (M) won eleven Assembly seats.

The origins of immigration into Assam began at the turn of the century when Assam's virgin lands were opened up for settlement by landless peasants from East Bengal. The immigration and settlements were not controlled. The influx that began with the building of the railway link between Assam and East Bengal was so huge that already by 1911 the Census Superintendent had anticipated some of the tensions that the flow was likely to generate, unless regulatory measures were taken up. The immigration, he noted, was "likely to alter permanently the whole future of Assam and to destroy more surely than the Burmese invaders of 1821 the whole structure of Assamese culture and civilization". It is impossible to appreciate the size of this influx without referring to concrete figures. The following table shows the population growth rate of Assam compared to that of the rest of the country:

Table 3.1 Population Growth Rate of Assam And India

Year	Assam	All-India
1901-11	16.8	5.7
1911-21	20.2	-0.3
1921-31	20.1	11.0
1931-41	20.5	14.2
1941-51	20.1	13.3
1951-61	35.0	21.6
1961-71	34.7	24.6

Analysing the census data for Assam during the period, the political scientist Myron Weiner has calculated that the migrant population and their descendants in 1971 were approximately 8.5 million as against an 'indigenous' population of 6.5 million. It is difficult to imagine any situation where such an influx would not cause social tensions and resentment, except perhaps under exceptional conditions of expanding economic opportunities such as that of the United States during boom periods. According to Gohain, the different communities in Assam "have been living as peaceable neighbours for generations" till suddenly the ruling classes decided to infuse a dose of "chauvinism" into the Assamese. Gohain is certainly right about the relations between Bengalis and Assamese, Hindus and Muslims in the pre-influx period. But what has developed in Assam as a consequence of the continued influx is not a composite society of peoples who mingle with one another, but a plural society of separate communities. It is the structuring effect of sudden demographic change rather than the "cultural weakness of the Assamese ruling elites", as Gohain alleges, which can better explain the "non-integration of the non-Assamese into Assamese society".

The concern with influx has had a long history in Assam's politics. In the face of local resentment, the British instituted the Line system in the 1920s, excluding certain tribal areas from the new settlers. There were protests against the inadequacy and inefficacy of the Line system. By the 1930s the influx became such a central concern in Assam that it even influenced the Assamese response to the nationalist movement and to the question of partition. Maulana Bhashani, the noted peasant leader from present-day Bangladesh, migrated to Assam in 1928. He demanded the abolition of the Line system and put forward the idea of a unified 'Bangasam' as a solution to the problem of East Bengali's landlessness. The Congress opposed the Muslim League's demand for unlimited immigration and promised an Assamese homeland within a federated India. They agreed to make 1938 a cut-off point and to provide all immigrants who came before that date with waste lands, where possible, after providing land to the local people. The Communist party too then supported that position. In the decade prior to Independence and partition, while the demand that Assam become part of Pakistan was mooted, "sponsored immigration" was initiated by the Muslim League government of Md Saadullah. The political instability in Assam during the decade prior to Independence, with seven elected government and a period of Governor's rule, was precipitated by nothing else but the influx issue. Popular memory is proverbially short. But if some people in Assam today find in the suggestion of 1971 as a cut-off point the farcical repetition of history, they cannot be blamed for having a relatively good memory.

The failure of Independence and partition to put a stop to the influx from East Pakistan (subsequently Bangladesh) is the major source of resentment underlying the present movement. The uninitiated might wish that the movement did not have a 'colonial' or 'linguistic' aspect to it. But such wishful thinking ignores the impact that the influx has already made on Assam's nationality question. Assam's tangled nationality question has often bewildered the outside observer. After the language riots in Assam in 1960, a confused Nehru asked in a public meeting in Guwahati the rhetorical question: "Where else but in Assam can Assamese be the official language?" To the applause of the crowd he derisively said: "In Bombay?" Yet in the context of the changed demographic reality in Assam and the emergence of a plural society, the question of the official language of Assam was far from self-evident. The riots on the issue bear bloody testimony to this. The applause of the crowd might have further confused Nehru. For little did he know that the meeting he was addressing was very likely to be attended only by the Assamese community. There were then three other major communities in Assam: the urban Bengali Hindus, the Muslim Bengali peasants and the hill peoples - most of whom later split away from Assam. While to the Assamese community anxious to defend themselves against the influx, the issue of Assam's official language acquired tremendous symbolic value, it succeeded in alienating the most indigenous of communities—the hill peoples who later constituted Meghalaya and Mizoram. The political leadership of the Bengali Muslim community skilfully insulated the influx issue from the language politics that dominated the scene by getting that community to return Assamese as their mother-tongue to the census enumerator. The language controversies in the state were therefore primarily conflicts between the Assamese and the urban Bengali Hindu communities. In the vastly changed demographic reality of Assam, the Assamese were now dependent on some bargaining with the other communities even to realize the dream of a linguistically defined Assamese homeland. Next to Jammu and Kashmir, Assam was a state where the majority linguistic community had the slightest of margins - they constituted a bare 57 per cent of the population in 1956. The slender majority only partly reflects the traditional diversity of the region.

It is important to note that a political arrangement between leaders of different communities was crucial to Assam's political stability since Independence. The political parties dependent on support across communities tacitly agreed not to raise this inconvenient issue. But they had hardly contributed to a genuine integration of the communities and the evolution of composite cultural patterns. That accounts for their total ineffectiveness in the current situation. While on the whole the politicians succeeded in putting a lid on the influx issue, it had occasionally burst into the open threatening a political crisis each time. In 1965 when relations with Pakistan were deteriorating, the state government under instructions from the centre activated the police and administrative machinery to expel Pakistani "infiltrators" and fixed June 1965 as the target date for expulsion. Hundreds were expelled. But the process had to be stopped when eleven MLAs protesting that Indian Muslims were harassed in the process threatened to resign. Major Assam politician such as Fakhruddin Ali Ahmed and Moinul Haque Chaudhuri left state politics and joined the centre as a result of deadlocks over the issue of repatriation of Pakistani infiltrators. As recently as 1971, in the struggle for Chief Ministership of the state, Mahendra Mohan Chaudhuri hinted that his main rival Moinul Haque Chaudhuri was a Pakistani national. That in the middle of the present events, the Janata government in Assam fell and the new government of J.N. Hazarika was unstable was no "extraordinary fluke" as Gohain puts it. It was the result of the collapse of the old consensus of leaders in the face of a popular movement of unprecedented proportions.

To understand Assam's events today, Assam's nationality question, tangled primarily as a result of the influx, would have to be accepted as real. That accounts for many of the contradictory aspects of the movement. There is no doubt that the foreigners' issue has driven a wedge across the communities more than any other issue in the past. Yet the present agitation in Assam led by students, which has engulfed the most distant of villages and primarily involving socio-cultural and literary bodies of the Assamese community, is nothing short of the Assamese civil society in rebellion. It is no middle-class movement. The so-called ambiguity in the term 'foreigner' reflects only the historically structured contradictions of a mass upsurge - primarily based on one community and oblivious of the demographic changes in Assam - which in highlighting an old issue is having to pretend that the divides of a plural society do not exist. Given the explosiveness of the issue, the movement has sought to pose the issue in secular terms. But such a secular definition in Assam's complex ethnic reality has only succeeded in increasing the insecurity of various communities. Social scientist and Marxists all over world are having to deal with complex ethnic realities that often co-exist with class realities. In some situations - South Africa being the most extreme example - it just will not do to say that the class reality is the only one. After all it is not the first time that a situation has arisen where Marxism has got mixed up with ethnic issues. In Lebanon, too, left and progressive ideas appear Islamic to the Christians. To suggest that Marxists and progressives should take ethnic realities seriously does not mean that they should support the present movement in Assam. They only should not leave the field wide open for those opposed to positive change to exploit. More concretely, they can build bridges across the communities in Assam, The basis for it, however, cannot be a confrontation with the movement with ill-founded slanders, which is bound to be construed as mere partisanship in Assam's ethnically polarized reality. Since there are many indications that there are many people in the Bengali Hindu and Muslim communities who want foreigners to be sent back, a genuine consensus of all communities on the issue can still be built. Unfortunately through Gohain's conspiratorial lenses those few healthy signs appear suspect. He alleges without any evidence that "members of minority communities were....forced to sign pledges and letters to the editor expressing total support to the cause of expelling foreigners". It is perhaps difficult for Gohain to imagine scenarios worse than the CPI (M) losing its eleven seats. It would be very unfortunate if that happens. But the scenario that bothers me more at this point is much worse: a deadlock in the negotiations between the central government and students, a total alienation of the Assamese community from the political process, increasing CRP violence, further worsening of relations between the communities while the left watches on with its increasingly irrelevant categories and further erosion of influence and a blood-bath in Assam.

4

Fall-out of Underdevelopment*

—Hiren Gohain

It is naturally difficult to supply irrefutable evidence of foreign complicity in the present agitation in Assam, though the circumstantial evidence is impressive. Besides, there is the danger of subjective bias. Our friends in the CPI think that the links forged by the movement with the Mizos and the Nagas are sufficient evidence to establish the involvement of China, though in my opinion such a reading is far-fetched.

The British are certainly worried over the prospect of labour unrest in the tea-gardens. They have a number of giant tea-plantations under their control and the marketing, even of the produce of Indian-owned tea-gardens, is dominated by Lipton and Brooke Bond. The British unease over growing labour unrest, now that the INTUC no longer enjoys a monopolistic position among the labour organization and there are everywhere signs of growing militancy, might well have led to the support of the managers to the movement in most cases. Significantly enough, the gardens were

* *EPW,* Vol. XV, No. 12, March 22,1980, pp. 589-90.

exempted from the several successful total Assam Bandhs organized by the Gana Sangram Parishad. The BBC has given immediate and wide coverage to the various phases of the movement. However, there is evidence that even before Independence the tea-planters had their 'own men' among the prominent political leaders of Assam, who had toyed with the idea of a 'sovereign' State of Assam if the British left (see Amalendu Guha, *From Planter-Raj to Swaraj,* Delhi, 1977).

As for the CIA there is little in terms of direct American investment in the economy. Of course, there is American collaboration in exploitation and extraction of Petroleum, but that does not amount to much. The more important reasons for any American involvement may well be strategic - a design to contain pro-Soviet forces, incarnate in the American eyes in the CPI (M)-led governments in West Bengal and Tripura. It is significant that when the movement was in its peak and there was a blind frenzy against the so-called "silent invasion" of the Bangladeshis, the Bangladesh border guards most conveniently started firing across the borders at Indian security forces! The recent success of the CPI (M) in assembly elections was a shot in the arm for the dirty tricks experts of the CIA.

Philip Agee's revealing account of the clandestine operations of the CIA ("Inside the Company", London, 1975) mentions certain features that are very much evident in the present movement in Assam: (1) A massive press-campaign against communists and Communism before an impending election; (2) Attempts to wreck "red" trade unions and create alternative non-communist unions; (3) Patronage to militant non-communist student movements.

The CIA is also supposed to be behind the sudden unanimity of views between the leaders of the hill tribes and the Assamese leaders. The history of their relations since Independence had been one of mistrust and *The Assam Tribune* had blandly advised bombing of the civilian population when the Indian Army had been foundering in Nagaland. The tribal organizations have apparently come under CIA influence through Christian missions, which have done much to earn their gratitude and affection. It is really odd that the chapter of misunderstanding and mistrust between the Assamese leaders and the leaders of the hill tribes should so abruptly be replaced by fraternizing and amiability.

During the late 1950s an influential work of American political science on India had been Selig T Harrison's "India: The Most Dangerous Decades", which predicted disintegration of the country and pointed among other things to Assamese linguistic fanaticism. It is clear that whenever the Indian economy and political life faces a crisis, the alternative for some time to come could hardly be the Left. In such a situation the regional forces have some chance. The CIA may well promote such forces to the point of secession provided it is in its interest.

Americans have recently taken some interest in the politics of this region. A well known American political scientist has also written a study of the "problem of migration" in this region. The CIA eggheads are quite likely to use the data collected by such investigations. In this they are a jump or two ahead of the security services of the Indian government, who do not seem to realize the potentiality of mischief in backwardness and frustration.

At the same time one must resist the temptation to pamper Fascist forces on the ascent in the North-East. Backwardness alone does not explain the shocking and widespread violence against the minorities, the brutal suppression of dissent in the local press, the anti-communist fury. Since the 1960s Assamese liberal middle-class culture has been undermined from within by a systematic infiltration of Fascist ideas and attitudes, so that the average educated Assamese is not shocked when the most reactionary and inhuman sentiments are purveyed by the local press in the guise of patriotism. There has indeed been a "treason of the intellectuals". They are so busy feathering their own nests, they don't seem to care when the ideals of humanism they profess are thrown overboard.

As for outsiders getting away with lucrative jobs and business opportunities, it is partly due to the lack of local skill and enterprise. First there is the objective situation failing to foster the virtues of steady diligence and thrift, hardy enterprise and punctuality. This is aggravated by the hangover of parasitical semi-feudal culture which promotes dreams of unearned leisure. This explains the educated Assamese attitude of contempt and coercion towards the labouring people of other races, who are expected only to be "hewers of wood and drawers of water" for their Assamese masters. This attitude has now percolated to the ranks of the Assamese peasantry.

The main reason for the widespread unemployment is of course underdevelopment. It is often forgotten that unemployment among the local Bengalis is much more acute than among the local Assamese. Hence progressives, instead of seeking to burden Bengalis with a false .sense of guilt, should strengthen the campaign to eliminate "uneven development". Besides, they should make it a point to fight resolutely all forms of bourgeois ideology that preach reactionary communism as an answer to fundamental economic ills. No doubt there is a remnant of Bengali chauvinism among sections of the local Bengali population, but that is hardly as great a danger as the virulent Assamese petty nationalism.

Has migration had no other effect than 'swamping Assamese identity' - as claimed by the Assamese opinion builders? Who built the roads and bridges that brought the different localities in Assam within reach of one another? Who staffed the first schools and colleges? Who started the first hospitals? Paradoxically enough, it was only the coming of skilled people from outside that indirectly laid the foundations of the Assamese 'national identity which is bandied about so freely by the Assamese leaders of the movement. The immigrant Muslim peasants from Eastern Bengal brought under the plough thousands of acres of swampy and uncultivable land, left fallow by the Assamese for generations. The trader from outside had helped in bringing inaccessible villages into contact with markets in the towns.

This is not to exonerate the Big Nation Chauvinism that influences the rulers in New Delhi. They do not seem concerned to encourage and develop the productive forces in the north-east, and appear interested in this region only as a hinterland for the manufacturers in metropolitan areas. This lopsided development must be corrected if Assam is not to turn into a threat to India.

5

Assam: A Colonial Hinterland*

—Tilottama Misra

A positive outcome of the nine-month old agitation on the foreigners' issue in Assam is the growing awareness among the Assamese people of being subjected to gross economic exploitation on a scale comparable to, and sometimes even worse than, in the pre-independence days. These days a great deal of writing on Assam and the North-East is devoted to the theme of colonial or 'quasi-colonial' exploitation of Assam by foreign imperialists and by the Indian State and the Indian big capitalists. Some of the writings have compared Assam's economic condition to that of the US South in the nineteen-thirties[1], and to East Pakistan before the creation of Bangladesh[2]. The general theme of most of the articles on the current movement published in newspapers and journals of Assam is that this state, rich in natural resources, has been progressively sucked dry of its wealth. Despite being the country's largest producer of tea, oil, plywood and forest products, Assam, is one of the poorest and industrially most backward states of India. India annually earns millions of rupees as foreign exchange from Assam's products, but the

* *EPW,* Vol. XV, No. 32, August 9,1980, pp. 1357-64.

per capita income (at current prices) of Assam in 1976-77 was only Rs. 816 (one of the lowest in India) as against the per capita National Income of Rs. 1,049 for that year. Manufactured goods from the metropolitan centres in other parts of the country are sold in Assam at three to four times their original price. About 23 per cent of the per capita income of Assam is spent in buying consumer goods from outside the state. Even for the smallest consumer articles, such as safety-pins and naphthalene balls, Assam has to look to other states. In a recent survey of this region carried out by the North-Eastern Industrial and Technical Consultancy Organization (1976), as many as 28 imported consumer goods were listed as articles that could be manufactured locally without market constraint[3].

These are some of the issues that have come up for discussion among various sections of the Assamese people today. A significant feature of the present movement in Assam is that it has gone a long way in disseminating views among the common people of the towns and villages of Assam about the colonial exploitation of the region. Even a semi-literate village woman can be seen discussing oil-royalty rates while she sits on the picket lines with college students and teachers. A brief survey of the colonial character of Assam's economy may, therefore, reveal telling facts that lie at the root of the present mass upheaval in the state.

It is interesting that the nature of most of the major industries of Assam - viz., tea, oil, plywood - is that of 'extractive enterprise' based on the abundant supply of raw material available in the state. In fact, industrially advanced powers invest capital in such enterprises in the colonies so that raw materials can be obtained for their industrialized countries[4]. There is hardly an industry in Assam that has been created by indigenous capital. Both oil mining and tea plantation were undertaken by British capitalists, and even today a major share of the investment in the Digboi refinery and in the tea plantations of the state represent foreign capital. After independence, surplus capital has been exported to Assam in the form of investment in tea and plywood by the Indian big bourgeoisie which has attained monopoly control over these industries. Without going into the ever controversial discussion centering round the exact nature of the Indian State and the relationship between the Centre and the states, it is possible to point out some of the characteristics of Assam's economy which fit in exactly with classical definitions of 'colonialism'. For example, E.G. Wakefield's argument regarding Britain's colonial policy was that "an industrialized State could generate surplus capital which it was unprofitable to invest at home either in agriculture or in industry (because foreign markets did not expand fast enough to absorb its products). This capital would be more profitably employed if it were exported to places where fertile land was in good supply. Provided ample labour was made available by emigration, capital would be now more productive in these new lands and at the same time would expand the market for British manufactures and increase the supply of cheap food-stuffs and industrial raw materials"[5]. Assam, too, has become an ideal market for manufactured goods from industrial parts of India and new industries and jobs have been created in cities outside Assam on the basis of products taken out of the state. It is significant that Guwahati is the only town in Assam which recently has been declared a Class-I town after the shifting of the capital from Shillong to Dispur. But, besides Guwahati, the only other town in Assam that has grown population-wise at a surprising rate in recent years is Tinsukia in upper Assam. Classed as a second category town in the 1971 Census, the population of this town had increased from 28,468 in 1961 to 54,911 in 1971 - a phenomenal rise of 92.89 per cent. The majority of this population, belongs to the trading communities such as the Rajasthanis, Punjabis and Biharis who are engaged in small business and in providing labour to the town's industrial establishments. Tinsukia also has a large concentration of Bengalis holding railway jobs and working as petty traders. Cut of over 500 shops in Tinsukia's main shopping center-the 'daily bazar' - only one or two are owned by local Assamese people[6]. The increase in Tinsukia's population is an indicator of the condition of the state's economy. Tinsukia is the terminus of the NF Railway and it is the only main town of Assam besides Guwahati which is on the main railway line of the state. So, it is economical for traders outside Assam to send manufactured goods directly to Tinsukia by rail. Tinsukia, therefore, has become the center for wholesale trade for entire upper Assam. The wholesale market in Tinsukia is controlled entirely by non-Assamese traders who are the agents of North Indian big businessmen, the retail market is in the hands of Marwaris, Biharis and Bengalis. A study of Tinsukia town, therefore, becomes a pointer to the general condition of trade and commerce in the whole of Assam.

It is necessary to study the existing conditions prevailing in some of the major extractive industries of Assam in order to understand how colonial exploitation is thriving in this state more than 30 years after British rule. As early as in 1834, soon after Assam lost her independence in 1826, the British began tea cultivation in Assam. The initial experiment was so successful that the British sought to establish full control and monopoly over this industry by forming the Assam Tea Company in 1840. Special rules, like the Waste Land Grant Rules of 1838, Old Assam Rules of 1854, Fee Simple Rules of 1862, Revised Fee Simple Rules of 1874, and New Lease Rules of 1876, enabled the British planters to own large tracts of the most fertile land of Assam at highly concessional rates. Under the Waste Land Grant Rules of 1838, for instance, one-fourth of the total land acquired for a tea garden could be enjoyed tax-free for life by the owner and even the rest of the land could be tax-free for periods varying from 5 to 20 years depending on the productivity of the soil. Thus, the British planters became the owners of almost seven lakh acres of tax-free land in Assam, while the local Assamese peasants paid two to three rupees per acre as land revenue to the British masters. "With the exception of lands settled for special cultivation under the New Lease Rules of 1876 and under the current special rules, lands granted under the older sets of rules were either wholly or partly revenue-free. Those under the Fee Simple Rules were fully revenue-free and one-fourth of the area of those under 45 years' Lease Rules, at 99 years' Lease Rules, were revenue-free in perpetuity. The owners of these lands had permanent, heritable and transferable rights....."[7]

Thus, even today, large areas of fertile tea-garden land are owned by British planters under the various concessional rules of the past. Since tea cultivation involved capital expenditure, so certain 'exceptional privileges'[8] were granted to the cultivators under the Waste Land Rules. But, these privileges were meant primarily for the British planters. Aspiring Assamese planters were discriminated against and discouraged from entering into competition with the British planters. The case of Maniram Dewan[9] was a typical example of the extent to which the British colonialists could go to prevent native enterprise in the tea business. When Maniram Dewan started the first private tea gardens in Assam, he displayed extraordinary skill, enterprise and business acumen which overshadowed the achievements of the Assam Tea Company formed initially with 10,000 shares of Rs. 500 each. What Maniram Dewan achieved in a short span of eight years, depending entirely on personal initiative, on individual capital, and on local Assamese labour aided by a few skilled Chinese hands, took almost 25 years for the British to achieve[10]. This, Maniram achieved in the face of severe obstacles put in his way by the British. The land that he acquired for the two tea-gardens at Cinnamora and Safrai was not granted special revenue concessions under the Waste Land Rules. On the other hand, his plantation land was assessed as ordinary rice-land, resulting in Maniram's having to pay very high rates of land revenue. It is evident from this that, during the initial stage of the colonization of Assam by the British, any competition from the local Assamese gentry in the sphere of tea was strongly discouraged. It is interesting that the main charges, of inciting rebellion against the British government, that were brought against Maniram Dewan were framed on the basis of several letters written to the government by the Assam Company, the Margherita Company and Nakchari Company. These letters alleged that Maniram and his followers were inciting the whole country against the British and that consequently the 'native contractors' were refusing to work in the British gardens[11].

After the consolidation of their economic hold over Assam, however, the British in the later part of the nineteenth century and early twentieth century did encourage a few Assamese planters to set up tea gardens on their own. Jagannath Barua (1851-1907) was the pioneer among this group of Assamese planters. But the number of tea gardens owned by these handful of Assamese planters were so few, and the total area of these gardens was such a small fraction of the total area under tea cultivation,[12] that they never could be a threat to British economic interests in this state. On the other hand, in line with the general British policy towards India after 1S57[13] this newly created Assamese bourgeoisie was considered a potential ally of the British administration. Maniram's success as a tea planter despite all obstacles, proves conclusively that it was not dearth of local enterprise and apathy towards business and industry that led to the almost total exclusion of the Assamese from the tea industry. Rather, the crippling conditions set by colonial exploitation of this region through a century and a half have pushed the people of this region far behind those of the rest of India. If the Assamese youth today is discontented at the monopoly by 'outsiders', over lucrative tea jobs, it is not because of a basic inferiority complex born out of a "lack of local skill and enterprise"[14]. The history of the Assam tea industry shows that, even at the time of its inception, the Bengali bourgeoisie from Calcutta were in an advantageous position. They entered the tea business as shareholders with the British colonialists, and enjoyed a share of the profits from the plantations they had never seen. It is on record that three out of the 11 members of the first set of Board of Directors of the Assam Tea Company were from Bengal. They were Dwarkanath Tagore, Motilal Sheel, and Prasanna Kumar Tagore. No wonder the people of Assam came to associate a section of the Bengali middle class with colonial exploitation in the tea industry.

The British made enormous profits from the tea industry in Assam. With a nominal capital investment, they kept the profit margin high by paying abominably low wages to the labourers brought almost as slaves from the poverty stricken areas of Bihar, Orissa and the Madras presidency. Though initially local Assamese people were employed as labourers, the practice was later discontinued because signs of rebellion and discontentment became evident among the Assamese labourers in those early years of the plantation days and the British could not risk an open conflict with the tribal population of Assam[15]. Immigrant labourers could be exploited and ill-treated without much impact on the surrounding villages. This practice, of discouraging local labour in tea plantation has been retained to this day. The British planters never invested a farthing in charitable organizations or welfare and developmental activities in the state. As has been pointed out by Homen Borgohain[16], not even a well was ever dug by the planters in villages surrounding the gardens nor was a rupee ever contributed by them for the establishment of a primary school in the region. Instead, the enormous profits from the Assam gardens enriched Britain and benefited British citizens. Even today, a large share of profits from the Assam gardens flow out freely to Britain and to the newly established British gardens in Africa, some of which have the same names as their Assam counterparts. Even today, the villages around the well-maintained beautiful gardens with their posh bungalows of the colonial days are some of the poorest in the region. Not that the situation is any better in the case of tea gardens owned by the big business groups such as Tatas and Birlas. When the British started selling some of their gardens after 1947, and especially after 1954 when there was a slump in the world tea prices, these gardens were bought over by Indian big capitalists because there were very few Assamese capitalists with such buying power and there was no public sector corporation at that time to buy up the gardens.

Today, out of about 620 tea gardens in the Brahmaputra Valley, only about 158 are owned by Assamese planters.

However, most of these gardens are small in size - some as small as 10-20 hectares only - and many do not even have their own factories. Of the remaining gardens, excluding 12 gardens owned by the newly-formed Assam Tea Corporation (a Government of Assam undertaking) and one owned by the Assam Tea Employees' Industrial Cooperative Limited, as many as 248 gardens are owned by the non-Assamese big bourgeoisie. Most of these are large and economically viable. According to the Monopoly Inquiry Commission of 1965, there are 24 factories in Assam belonging to the top 75 business groups in the private sector and almost all these factories are located in the tea gardens. There are, technically speaking, no foreign companies in the tea business at present after the rupeeisation of the sterling companies. But there are about 175 Agency House gardens in Assam with foreign capital involved and most of these are large concerns whose stated gross profits range from Rs. 1 crore to 12 crore. For example, in 1976, the gross profits of the Duncan Agro-Industries Limited were Rs. 4.69 crore while that of Tata Finlay and Macneill-Magor were Rs, 12.24 crore and Rs. 7.93 crore, respectively[17].

The transfer of ownership of a large number of tea gardens from British to Indian capitalist hands has had little perceptible effect on the economic life of the Assamese people. The only difference, much in evidence today, is that while the British in their own interests employed local hands both in the managerial and clerical posts (particularly in the latter), the Indian big capitalist have started to bring people from other parts of the country to fill up all categories of posts. These people, in most cases, have almost no acquaintance with the planting and processing of tea - their only claim to the tea-jobs happens to be their 'connections'. Today, one rarely comes across an Assamese manager or assistant-manager in gardens owned by Indian capitalists. The Fifth Report of the Employment Review Committee (1976), set up by the Assam Assembly, makes revealing reading:

A comparative study between the gardens under the four different Associations reveals that, so far as the representation of local people in the managerial cadre (including assistant managers) is concerned the position is the worst in respect of the tea gardens under the Tea Association of India, where 82 per cent of posts in the managerial cadre have been held by persons with birthplaces outside Assam. It may be noted that almost all gardens under the membership of TAI are owned by Indians after the take-over of ownership from the European management. One striking point to be noted is that, after change-over to Indian management, almost all the posts in the managerial cadre (including assistant managers) were filled up by persons from outside the state of Assam without any open advertisement or without notifying to employment exchange (Report of the Employment Review Committee, 1976, p. 162).

It is significant that while the majority of the managerial posts under the Assam Branch of the Indian Tea Association, the Tea Association of India and the Bharatiya Chah Parishad are held by people from outside the state in the gardens under the Assam Tea Planters Association (Brahmaputra Valley), nearly 67 per cent of such posts are held by people from within the state. The head office of the ATPA is in Jorhat and this Association was formed in the 1939s on the initiative of some eminent Assamese planters like Nabin Chandra Bordoloi and R.K. Baruah. The head office of the ITA, TAI and BCP, however, are all situated outside Assam. In the pattern of employment prevailing in these head offices one may discern the general pattern of employment in the managerial cadre of the gardens affiliated to these Associations. For example, out of the 20 office bearers in the head office of the ITA at Calcutta in 1972-73, 17 were from Calcutta itself and one each from New Delhi, Jalpaiguri and Assam.

The total annual profit from the tea gardens of Assam is several times more than the total annual revenue receipts of the state. The state of Assam is entitled to an agriculture tax imposed on 60 per cent of the profit from the tea gardens, while the Central government is entitled to an income-tax on 40 per cent of the total profit. But there is ample ground to believe that it has become a common practice with both the Indian and the foreign capitalists to conceal the major share of their profits, thus robbing the state government as well as, the Centre of their due share of the revenue and taxes[18]. Moreover, though the 756 tea gardens of Assam account for about 55 per cent of the tea produced in India and earn an annual Rs. 500 crore as foreign exchange for the country, except for the newly-formed Assam Tea Corporation which is a public sector organization owning a few sick and unprofitable gardens, the overwhelming majority of the big gardens are under foreign and Indian companies which are controlled from London and Calcutta. Assam did not have a tea auction center till a few years ago, and even when the only one it now has was opened at Guwahati, the move was opposed by Left leaders such as Jyoti Basu. Even the main office of the Tea Board, which is the highest authority in relation to the tea industry and which besides implementing the Tea Act of 1958 is also responsible for approving grants, loans, and labour-welfare projects, is situated in Calcutta though most of the gardens it controls are in Assam. Thus the demand for the nationalization of the tea industry in Assam, the shifting of the head offices of the tea companies to Assam thereby providing jobs for the people of Assam, and the continuing deplorable working condition of the tea labourers, cannot be dismissed as merely 'parochial' demands but must be seen as reactions against the protracted colonial exploitation in the tea sector.

As a fall-out of the current mass movement in Assam, the demand has been raised for the sale of the entire quantity of tea produced in Assam at the Gauhati tea-auction center, because all these years the state has been losing revenue from sales-tax on its tea since the major portion of the tea is still sold in the Calcutta Auction, The leading buyers of the Gawahati Tea Auction have pointed out that Assam gets only Rs. 22 crore for the tea produced in the state whereas West Bengal gets Rs. 42 crore as sales tax for the tea from the Assam gardens auctioned in Calcutta[19]. This interesting fact has been brought to the notice of the Lok Sabha by Jyotirmoy Basu of the CPI (M) during the current Lok Sabha session while he was speaking on the Appropriation Bill of the Assam Budget[20]. Basu also pointed out in the course of his speech that, for the plywood extracted from the state, Assam gets only Rs. 35 lakhs whereas the Central government gets Rs. 80 crore.

Assam has an estimated reserve of 70.46 million tonnes of crude oil and 23,000 million cubic metres of natural gas. About 43 lakh tonnes of crude is produced by the oilfields of upper Assam and since this crude has a very high percentage of aromatic content, it is rated high in the world market. According to international price standards, Assam crude should cost at least 1.5 times more than the low grade OPEC crude. But despite possessing such a valuable non-replenishable resource, Assam's economy, unlike that of other oil-rich countries, gets little from its oil. The British established the small private sector refinery at Digboi, which still represents foreign investment. But the Government of India has to date stubbornly resisted all demands for a sufficiently large public sector refinery near the oil-rich areas of upper Assam. The suggestion put forward by Soviet experts, on the basis of extensive surveys, for the establishment of a large-scale refinery at Silghat near Nowgong was rejected outright. There could have been no other reason except vested political interests for the establishment of the large public sector refinery for Assam crude at Barauni with an annual capacity of more than 30 lakh tonnes. Mass movements protesting against this unfair decision of the Centre were staged in Assam in 1956-57, as a result of which the Centre tried to appease the people by establishing a small refinery at Guwahati with an annual refining capacity of only about 7 lakh tonnes. For more than 12 years after that, the simple-minded Assamese remained euphoric seeing a refinery being constructed at last on Assam soil. But when the deceit of the Centre became evident, another mass movement shook the state in 1969, demanding the setting up of a second public sector refinery in the state. But even this time the new refinery-cum-petrochemical complex fell far short of the size and capacity of the Barauni refinery, its refining capacity being only about 10 lakh tonnes a year. It has also been alleged that the naphtha-cracking unit of this complex has already been transferred to the planned Mathura refinery. The site for the conversion of polyester fibre into yarn may be shifted from the Bongaigaon complex because of alleged delay and apathy of the present Government of Assam in replying to the letter of intent from the Ministry of Petroleum[21]. Even more intriguing, the kerosene produced in the refineries of Assam is carried by a product pipe-line all the way to Siliguri, where the marketing division of this product of Assam is situated, and it is distributed from there for the consumption of the north-eastern states. There is thus quite often acute shortage of kerosene in the villages and towns surrounding the oil refineries of Assam, even when the refineries are running full swing. Also the sales tax on the kerosene from Assam goes to West Bengal and not to this state[22]. Even this perhaps would not have rankled among the Assamese so much, had Assam been given her due share of royalty on the crude produces. This is today Rs. 42 per tonne. Recently, the Government of Assam submitted a memorandum to the Centre demanding the revision of oil royalty rates from Rs. 42 to Rs. 315 per tonne of crude with effect from January 1976. It was argued in the memorandum that, since crude was a non-replenishable commodity, "the proprietors of this natural resource should be adequately compensated". Assam has lost sizeably up to the end of last year (1979) because the Government of India has refused to fix the royalty rates on Assam crude at 20 per cent of the posted price of equivalent Middle East crude in India. It was further pointed out in the government's memorandum that, even the sales tax that Assam derives from her crude is Rs. 54 per tonne, whereas India gets Rs. 991 per tonne as sales tax on Assam crude. This well argued proposal of the Assam government, which came in the wake of the current movement in the state has been rejected outright by the Centre. Although international oil prices are going up every year, Assam's oil royalty will not be increased even by a rupee. It is unfortunate that there is little public opinion in the rest of India against this gross injustice done to Assam although much concern is shown about the loss to the country due to the oil blockade resorted to by the people of Assam.

The growing importance of natural gas as a source of energy and as raw material for a variety of modern industries does not seem to impress the Central government much. For, over 50 million cubic feet of natural gas is being flared off daily at the different oilfields of Assam for several decades. In 1978, only about 848 million cubic meters of gas was utilized in Assam and most of it went to the Namrup thermal plant. It is intriguing that the Central government should allow the natural gas to be burnt up as waste when its proper utilization would have turned Assam into one of the richest states regarding power generation, production of various industrial goods like different types of rubber, plastics, nylon and polyester fibres, paints, dyes, lacquer, pesticides and a variety of other chemicals. Due to the almost total non-utilisation of the natural gas and the by-products of the crude refined in Assam, no ancilliary industries have been set up in Assam while such industries dependent on the raw material from the Assam oilfields are multiplying at a rapid rate in the metropolitan centers of India.

Another extractive industry is the plywood industry of Assam. For, 80 per cent of the produce of the 40 large plywood factories of Assam is transferred by road and rails to depots outside Assam. Not a single sales depot for plywood is situated within Assam though the state produces several lakh cubic meters of plywood. There are 14 sales depots at Ahmedabad, Bangalore, Bombay, Chandigarh, Dhanbad, Gudgaon, Hyderabad, Indore, Jaipur, Jullunder, Madras, Nagpur, New Delhi, and Benares, for the four plywood factories of Assam owned by the Birla Group. Not a single plywood factory is owned either by the local people or by the state government and, till May 1979, not a single agency for plywood was given to anyone from Assam. Only 15 plywood factories of the state produce tea-chests for the tea gardens of Assam and they produce only 50 per cent of the total requirement of these gardens. Most of the plywood factories sell their tea-chests through their agents in Calcutta. Gross discrimination against the local people of Assam is evident even in the case of employment in the plywood factories. Of the highly paid jobs in the managerial category, more than 76 per cent of the recruitment is from outside the state while more than 42 per cent of the lower category job-holders are also from other parts of the country. Since it is not the general practice with the management of the plywood factories to advertise their posts or keep in touch with the local employment exchanges, so out of the 6,489 employees in the plywood factories of Assam only about 1.1 per cent have been employed through the employment exchange. Thus the local people of Assam have been deprived of their rightful claim to jobs in the plywood factories. Besides, it is alleged that, every year, the plywood factories of Assam deal in a clandestine manner with plywood worth Rs. 12 to 15 lakhs. Thus the rich forest wealth of Assam is diminishing fast to swell the purses of unscrupulous big business from outside the state. How the entire ecological balance of the state is being adversely affected by this indiscriminate felling of trees would be the matter for another study[23].

Besides these three extractive industries - viz., tea, oil and plywood - Assam has no other major industry except the public sector fertilizer factory at Namrup. The Namrup plant produced 153.9 thousand tonnes of fertilizer in 1977-accounting for about 45 per cent of the total output of the Hindustan Fertilizer Corporation. The production of the Namrup plant is expected to increase further with the commissioning of a third plant. As it is, the Namrup unit is the largest in Hindustan Fertilizer Corporation. Yet, the headquarters of the HFC is proposed to be set up in Calcutta, notwithstanding the repeated requests of the Assam Government to locate it within Assam. Similarly, the headquarters of the Hindustan Paper Corporation have been set up in Calcutta in utter disregard of the legitimate claims of

Assam that, since three of the four plants of the HPC are located in Assam, the headquarters of the HPC should be located in the state.

Jute textile is listed as an important industry of Assam in the *Economic Survey* published by the state government. In 1976-77, 105.3 thousand hectares of land in Assam was under jute cultivation, yielding over 7 lakh bales of jute. Jute production in the state which fell alarmingly from over 11 lakh bales in 1973-74 to 7 lakh bales within just a year did, however, register an increase to over 9 lakh bales in 1978-79. The fall in the area under jute cultivation was partly the result of distress sale of raw jute by farmers in the 1973-74 drought in Assam and partly owing to the arbitrary fixation of raw jute prices by private traders who have monopoly control over the jute business. The Jute Corporation of India and the STATFED procure only about 15 to 20 per cent of the total jute produced in the state. Moreover, even in the price fixation by the JCI, there is no uniformity in prices for the same quality jute produced by Assam and West Bengal. Good quality Assam jute was bought by JCI at Rs. 175 per quintal in 1978, while West Bengal jute was bought at Rs. 225 per quintal. West Bengal, Assam and Bihar are the only three jute producing states of India producing together, the highest quantity of jute in the world. But only about 4.2 thousand tonnes of jute textiles are produced in Assam. There were 68 jute mills in operation in 1978 and of these 56 were situated in West Bengal, four in Andhra Pradesh, three in Bihar, three in Uttar Pradesh, one in Madhya Pradesh, and one in Assam. If jute mills can be established in states that do not produce any jute at all, only one jute mill in a state which produces a major share of the country's jute helps to prove the Centre's colonial policy towards Assam.

The industrial backwardness of the state can be gauged to a certain extent by the number of registered factories and the average number of workers employed daily. According to Assam government figures, there were only 1,782 registered factories in Assam in 1977, employing about 82,000 workers daily. Most of these are tea-garden factories. The number of joint stock companies in Assam is even less. While there were 44,000 such companies in the whole of India in 1975-76, in Assam there were only 635 till that year - less than 1.5 per cent of the all-India average. As regards commercial manufacturing firms, Assam draws an almost complete blank. The enormity of the situation can be understood by leafing through some 300 pages of the Times of India Directory Yearbook (1979) giving the list of the thousands of commercial firms in the country. Only after patient search through the masses of names can about 15 names of commercial firms be spotted in Assam. These are engaged in manufacturing minor products on a small scale. The only firm among these that can be taken note of is the Ashok Paper Mills in Goalpara. There is not a single firm manufacturing polythene bags or plastic containers and other such products made from petroleum wastes. It was in the course of the present movement in Assam that the people of the state became aware that several polythene industries in Bombay were on the verge of being closed down because of the oil blockade in Assam. Nor is there a single silk or art silk mill in Assam with more than 24 power looms - though Assam produced 187,000 kg of raw silk and 89,000 kg of silk yarn in 1976-77. Total production of raw silk in the country in that year was 3.268 thousand kg. Assam is the fifth large producer of mulberry silk in India and the whole of the North-Eastern region produces 90 per cent of the raw silk of the *Endi* variety. Moreover, Assam is the sole producer of the coveted golden *Muga* silk in the world. An estimated 53,000 kg *of Muga* raw silk is produced in the state annually. Despite such large production of raw silk, no steps whatsoever have been taken by the government to organize the silk industry on a sound commercial footing. The silk growers of the state are being increasingly exposed to the mercy of traders from other parts of the country who monopolies the business of processing and spinning of raw silk.

According to the *Economic Survey* (1977-78) published by the Government of Assam, the slow pace of industrial development in the state is "due to lack of requisite economic infrastructure and inherent inhibitions". Although the second reason put forward is obscure, the first is clearly evident from the poor state of banking facilities, transport, communication, power generation and consumption in the state. There were only 354 bank offices in Assam till June 1976, with total bank deposits aggregating just Rs. 134 crores. Bank credit was a meager Rs. 64 crores. The Table gives the comparative figures of some states.

Table 5.1: Distribution of bank offices, deposits and credits

State	*Bank Offices Per Lakh of Population*	*Per Capita Bank Deposit (Rs.)*	*Per Capita Bank Credit (Rs.)*
Andhra Pradesh	3.8	150	103
Assam	2.0	79	38
Bihar	1.9	112	49
Gujarat	6.1	367	201
Haryana	5.3	202	112
Karnataka	6.5	228	226
Kerala	7.0	203	144
Madhya Pradesh	2.6	94	48
Maharashtra	4.7	576	443
Orissa	2.1	56	30
Punjab	8.3	487	156
Raj as than	3.5	104	65
Tamil Nadu	5.0	225	268
Uttar Pradesh	2.8	146	66
West Bengal	3.2	370	255

Source: *Basic Statistics on Indian Economy,* Volume 1, December 1977.

In the field of power generation too, Assam is low down in the all-India list. Although there is a large potential of hydel power in Assam - a state crisscrossed by fast mountain streams and rivers - there is not a single hydroelectric generating plant in Assam at present. There are only two thermal generating plants at Chandrapur (30 mw) and

Namrup (115 inw) and a few diesel generating stations producing about 15 mw of power. The total generating capacity of all these plants was only 156 mw till 1977 (Source: ASEB). But most of the other Indian states such as Andhra, Gujarat, Kerala, Maharashtra, Tamil Nadu, UP and West Bengal, have each more than 1,000 mw installed capacity of power generation. A glance at the Energy (thermal and nuclear) map of India shows that there are seven such major power projects for the Northern Region with an additional seven under construction, nine for the Western Region with an additional three under construction, three for the Southern Region, eight for the Eastern Region with an additional nine more under construction. Most of these power projects have generating capacity of up to 600mw. But there is only one such project for the entire North-Eastern Region with only 115mw capacity, while another with a capacity of 120 mw is under construction at Bongaigaon. No wonder the per capita power consumption and the figure for rural electrification of the North-East is the lowest in the entire country.

, The sadly inadequate transport facilities in Assam is another cause for the slow pace of economic development of the state. Even 30 years after independence the whole of the North-East comprising the states of Assam, Meghalaya, Nagaland, Manipur, Mizoram, Arunachal Pradesh and Tripura has only 2,215 km of railway line. Uttar Pradesh alone has 8,706 km, MP has 5,735 km and Gujarat 5,607 km. Some of the North-Eastern states like Mizoram, Manipur, Arunachal Pradesh and Meghalaya are not linked at all by rail with the rest of India. Nagaland has a bare 9 km of railways. Assam was not linked by broad-gauge railway with the rest of India till recently. A mere 105 km of broad-gauge line were constructed after mass agitations in the state; but after several years of its construction, Guwahati, the only one of the two main towns of Assam on the main railway line, is yet not touched by broad-gauge. The construction work of the broad-gauge line between Guwahati and New Bongaigaon was started in 1976 and was scheduled for completion in 1978-79.

But, after the initial allotment of Rs 2 crore only, the project was downgraded and only Rs 1.5 crore were allotted for 1977-78. In the succeeding year's budget, too, only Rs 2.48 crore were allotted when the total requirement for completion of work was at least Rs 30 crore. As a result, little progress has been made on the work till this year and there appears to be little chance of the work being completed in the near future.

The British constructed the existing metre-gauge railway line in Assam in 1881 to facilitate the transportation of tea and troop movements whenever necessary. So, Assam's single main railway line passes through the tea-belt of the state without touching most of the important towns and villages. It is interesting that, even today, important Assam towns like Nowgong, Jorhat, Sibsagar, and Dibrugarh, are connected only by branch lines and there is no direct rail link between these towns. The railway map of Assam has remained the same since the British days, and the motives which impelled the British to construct the railway in this region appear to be shared by the administrators from Delhi. Passenger comfort naturally comes lowest in the list of priorities of the NF Railway which is primarily devoted to the transportation of Assam's natural resources to industries located outside the state.

The current movement in Assam has not only focused on the deplorable state of rail communication in the North Eastern Region but has also highlighted the pattern of employment in the railways and other services, a pattern which seems to have continued since the British days. The British had brought into Assam, during the initial years of their rule, people from outside the state - particularly from Bengal-to man the various services. But even after two decades of independence and the existence of Assam as a separate state, the Employment Review Committee, set up by the Assam Assembly, reveals the following:

> Till the time of collecting the last phase of data on 21st February, 1976, the NF Railway headquarters at Maligaon had in all 4,474 employees of whom nearly two-thirds (59 per cent) had their birthplaces outside Assam. Of the total number of

employees only 1,830 accounting for 41 per cent had their birthplaces in Assam (p. 17).

Another fact recorded by the committee is that, among the 2,644 employees of the NF Railway Headquarters at Maligaon with birthplaces outside Assam, the bulk (1,504) are from erstwhile Dhaka (now Bangladesh) accounting for 57 per cent, followed by 22 per cent for West Bengal. It has been further recorded that employees with Bengali as mother tongue predominate all classes of jobs, from Class I to Class IV, accounting for 60 per cent of the total employees. Employees with Assamese as their mother-tongue constituted only 28 per cent[24].

This brief survey of the colonial pattern of exploitation of Assam's resources should throw some light on one's understanding of the cause behind the large-scale and sustained participation of both rural and urban masses in the current movement in the state. A common charge being levelled against the Assam movement is that it has been diverting the attention of the masses from the basic problem of economic under-development of the North-Eastern Region. On the contrary, as the movement is becoming a protracted one, Assam's hydra-headed economic problems are drawing greater attention from the conscious section of the Assamese public. While the foreign nationals' issue[25], which is primarily centred around the ownership of land is spreading in the rural areas, the urban people have started seeing the problem as one of industrial underdevelopment, a fall-out of the colonial pattern, resulting in poverty and large-scale unemployment.

That Assam is nothing but a colonial hinterland for the industrial centers of India is the theme of most writings and public speeches of the Assamese intelligentsia involved in the movement. This growing consciousness among the Assamese middle class has been further heightened by the provocative and insensitive statements made by the Central leaders and a section of the national Press regarding the Assam movement. There has been an unusually sharp and prompt reaction to all this as conclusive evidence of what is being described as a 'hostile and colonial' attitude of the Indian ruling class towards the North Eastern Region. Therefore, the problem that is rocking Assam today is more deep-rooted than it appears to the rest of India from a distance.

It is generally admitted today that the movements for self-determination (economic and political) of the oppressed and backward nationalities of India cannot be dismissed as merely parochial and chauvinist outbursts aided and abetted by foreign agencies. That they are the result of certain internal contradictions of the Indian nation is now an accepted fact. These demands for autonomy and independence are generally characterized by strong reactions against 'outsiders', because for the common people of these exploited regions the 'outsider' very often appears as the most tangible symbol of colonial rule. A lasting solution of the Assam problem, therefore, would require serious re-thinking on the entire question of balanced regional development and a radical re-orientation of the Centre's economic policies towards this region.

REFERENCES

1. Sarma, Parameswar: 'A Region of Neglected Potentialities and Unrealised Opportunities', in : *Assam and the Assamese Mind,* Assam Sahitya Sabha, Jorhat, 1980.
2. For examples refer to *Himmat,* April 18, 1980; Nibaran Bora, in *Nagarik* (Assamese) December 15, 22, 29, 1977, reprinted in the same weekly in May 1980. *Nagarik is edited* by Homen Borgohain.
3. Sarma, Parameswar: *op. cit.,* p. 102.
4. Kautsky, John H: 'An Essay in the Politics of Development', in *Political Change in Underdeveloped Countries,* New York, 1963, p. 22.
5. Fieldhouse, D. K: 'Colonialism: Economic Aspect' in: *International Encyclopedia of Social Sciences,* Volume 3.
6. *Indian Express* (Delhi edition), May 23, 1980.
7. Das, J.N: *An Introduction to the Land Laws of Assam,* Guwahati, 1973, p. 6.
8. Baden-Powell, B.H: *The Land Systems of British India,* Volume 3, Delhi, 1974, p. 410.

9. Maniram Dewan an astute politician, was a Minister to the Ahom King, Purandar Singha. After the British entered Assam in 1826, he became an important adviser to the British and brought to their notice the possibility of the commercial cultivation of tea which was then growing wild in the Singhpho area. When the Assam Tea Company was formed by the British, Maniram Dewan was appointed its adviser in 1839 by virtue of his specialized knowledge of tea. According to Samuel Baildan, "various merchants in Calcutta were discussing the chance of imported Chinese (tea) seed thriving in Assam, when a native from the province present, seeing some tea seeds said. 'We have the plant growing wild in our jungles'. This was Maniram Dewan, the first native next to the then Raja of Assam - a very rich man with plenty of local influence" [Quoted by Benudhar Sarma in *Maniram Dewan* (Assamese), p. 971. Maniram Dewan helped the British Company to establish its first tea-garden in Assam. In 1845, he resigned from the Assam Tea Company and set up two gardens on his own. He was sentenced to death in 1858 by the British for his complicity with the 1957 revolutionaries. After his execution, both his tea gardens were taken over by the British.
10. Sarma, Benudhar: *Maniram Dewan* (Assamese), Guwahati, Second edition, p. 110.
11. *Ibid., p.* 175.
12. For example, the total area of the 14 gardens owned by the Assamese planters in the Sibsagar District was about 8,160 acres, while the Assam Tea Company alone had 40, 202 acres, Jorhat Tea Company had 14,654 acres and Singlo Tea Company had 13,828 acres. *(Assam District Gazetteers,* Volume 7, Sibsagar, 1906). For details see Hiren Gohain, *Asamiya Madhyabitta Samajar Itihas,* Natun Prithibi, Guwahati, 1972-73.
13. Metcalf, Thomas R. : *The Aftermath of Revolt,* India, 1857-1S70, OUP, 1965, Chapter 7.
14. Gohain, Hiren: *EPW,* March 22,1980.
15. Guha, Amalendu: *Planter - Raj to Swaraj,* ICHR, 1977, p. 15.
16. Borgohain, *Homen Aupanibeshik Soshanar Biruddhe Asomar Sesh Sangram* (Assamese), Guwahati, 1980, p. 64.
17. *ibid.,* p. 44.
18. *Ibid,* pp. 43-47,
19. *The Assam Tribune,* Guwahati, June 16,1980.
20. *The Assam Tribune,* Guwahati, June 15,1980.
21. *The Assam Tribune,* Guwahati, June 15,1980.

22. Since the commissioning of the Guwahati-Siliguri products-pipeline, one of the longest such pipelines in the world, West Bengal has earned, till 1979, several crores as levy on the petroleum products of Assam.
23. All the facts relating to the plywood industry in Assam are taken from the findings of a Review Committee set up by the Assam Assembly in 1978. This Committee led by Nagen Barua had submitted a detailed report before the Borbora government.
24. *Report of the Employment Review Committee,* Assembly Secretariat, Dispur, 1976, p. 23.
25. This point has also been dealt with by Gail Omvedt in 'Aspects of the Assamese Problem', *Frontier,* Calcutta, June 7, 1980.

6

Little Nationalism Turned Chauvinist Assam's Anti-Foreigner Upsurge, 1979-80*

—Amalendu Guha

Not being convinced that Assam's so-called anti-foreigner movement is a cudgel of chauvinism, Gail Omvedt raises some pertinent questions in *EPW,* March 12, 1980 and she herself answers these in *Frontier,* June 7, 1980, In the wake of the movement, the month of January saw an anti-Bengali pogrom in North Kamrup. In March she suggests that, to understand the events correctly, we need an analysis of "the fundamental class/national characteristics of the society and the movement" as well as of the "objective basis" for the autochthons' fear that "they and their cultural-national identity may be swept by the Bengali influx". She almost jumps to the conclusion - and this without the necessary homework - that the agitation is one of national self-determination. In her June article, she further says:

> The basic Assamese fear is not so much of losing jobs to Bengalis (or other 'outsiders') but of losing their land. This is a much more

* *EPW,* Vol. XV, No. 41-43, Special Number, October, 1930, pp. 1699-1720.

basic issue, because it calls into question one of the defining characteristics of a nationality that of a territory; and the loss of territory to people who settle on it tends to be permanent.

In his articles in *EPW,* March 15 and May 17, 1980, Sanjib Baruah, too, refuses to take note of the chauvinist and middle class character of the Assam movement and holds that, despite contradictions, it is in essence a legitimate, non-violent and peaceful rebellion of the Assamese civil society for self-expression. Like Gail Omvedt, Baruah too rationalizes the agitation in terms of supposed dangers from the Bengali influx to the autochthons' cultural-national identity, but with one difference. He avoids the term "self-determination", and prefers to talk of Assamese sub-nationalism. This is understandable. For, his frame of reference is not multinational India in the Marxist style, but India's "plural society", a concept borrowed from the neocolonialist social scientists - Chicago sociologists and Cambridge historians, for example - who attempt to deny usefulness of such categories as class and nationalism in the case of third world countries like India.

Yet another contributor to *EPW,* August 9, 1980, Tilottama Misra, highlights the movement as one essentially set against extra-regional big business domination over the region's economy. Over the months the movement has been able, she says, to make the common people aware of the big business stranglehold being the cause of economic underdevelopment. According to her, the present exploitation of Assam is in no way different from what one experienced in the colonial period; it now reflects the domination of a small nationality by the rest of India. Misra's is an attempt to provide the economic rationale for what she passes as a popular struggle for self-determination.

In an attempt to understand the Assam movement in relation to the national question, we shall take up the issues raised by the above-mentioned authors and offer our own comments. Throughout this article, we shall mean by the term

'Assamese' all inhabitants who have their domicile in the present Assam, whether of origin or of choice; and by the term 'Asamiya', those amongst them who profess Asamiya to be their natural or acquired mother tongue. Thus, the neo-Asamiyas, i.e. those immigrants and tribal autochthons who have adopted Asamiya as their language are also covered by the term 'Asamiya', unless otherwise stated. Little nationalism is defined by us as a spiritual sentiment that holds together a group of people claiming a common cultural-regional identity (to distinguish themselves from the other groups) and desirous of a degree of autonomy within the larger nation-state. India continues to be a melting pot of several yet-unconsolidated nationalities which simultaneously tend to merge with each other. Hence, one has to take note of the flexibility of the situation and avoid ascribing finality to any national formation, as it is found today, within the larger concept of the growing Indian nationhood.

I

Assamese Society: Its National and Class Characteristics

The present State of Assam as well as the horizon of the Assamese society is much larger than what it was under the Ahom Kings. During the last hundred years of its existence, or even before, the Ahom Kingdom of Assam did not include the districts of Goalpara, Cachar and the North Cachar Hills within its territory. After its annexation in 1826 to British India, the erstwhile Ahom territory or Assam Proper (i.e. Kamrup, Nowgong, Darrang, Lakhimpur, Dibrugarh and Sibsagar districts) became a new Division of the Bengal Presidency. Later, during 1874-1947, it used to form part of a separate Province - an amalgam of Asamiya-speaking, Bengali-speaking and myriad-tongued hills tribal areas - in which Asamiya was the claimed mother tongue of less than a quarter and Bengali of more than 40 per cent of the population.

Table 6.1: Mother tongue-wise distribution op population in Assam, 1971

Language Group	*Brahmaputra Valley*		*Autonomous Hills Area*	*Cachar District*	*Total State*	
	Population (1000)	*% to Total Population*	*Population (1000)*	*Population (2000)*	*Population (1000)*	*Language group as % to Total Population*
Asamiya	8,844	71.0	54	7	8,905	60.9
Bengali	1,502	12.0	48	1,332	2,882	19.7
Hindi	567	4.5	32	193	792	5.4
Bodo	499	4.0	33	2	534	3.7
Nepali	316	2.5	29	4	349	2.4
Karbi	18	0.1	172	1	121	1.3
Oriya	133	1.0	3	14	150	1.0
Sub- total	11,879	95.3	371	1553	13,803	94.4
Other Languages	3,613	4.7	84	160	822	5.6
Total population	12,457	(100)	455	1,713	14,625	100

Source : *Curiaus of India* 1971, Series 3 Assom Part 1-A General Report, Table VII, 2, p. 91 and Series 1, Part II, C(i), Social and Cultural Tables, Table C-V-B.

As a result of the progressive reorganization of the state during 1947-1972, on the basis of the linguistic principle, the State of Assam today is 61 per cent Asamiya-speaking, another 8 per cent speaking indigenous tribal languages. However, 99.3 per cent of the state's Asamiya-speakers are concentrated in the districts of the Brahmaputra Valley, which homeland they share with tribal autochthons spread over pockets of concentration. In each of the two other regions - (i) the hills region enjoying a degree of autonomy under the Sixth Schedule of our Constitution (i.e., the districts of Karbi Anglong and North Cachar Hills) and (ii) the outlying district of Cachar - the Asamiyas constitute an insignificant linguistic minority (as the Bengalis do in two subdivisions of Darjeeling in West Bengal). In Cachar, their home district, Cachar-Bengalis constitute 78 per cent of the population while the Asamiyas there account for LESS than 0.05 per cent. Besides, there are other minorities as well, such as the Meiteis. The tangled national question of Assam cannot be comprehended unless this historically, evolved regional-cultural pattern is constantly kept in mind (see Table 1).

It was Anandaram Dhekial Phukan (1829-59) who, first, talked of an Assamese 'nation' and made language the unifying symbol of its modern national consciousness. He also saw it as a member of the Indian family of nationalities. Of the 89 lakh Asamiya-speakers of India in 1971, 99.4 per cent were enumerated in Assam. Only 6 per cent of the Asamiya speakers live in towns as against a corresponding 18 per cent in the case of the state's Bengalis. The gap would have been much narrower if the village-dwelling Muslim immigrants from East Bengal, who adopted Asamiya as their language, were not accepted as Asamiyas and deemed as Bengalis. These indices of spatial immobility and low urbanization are nevertheless revealing. Because of a retarded and distorted economic growth under Colonial conditions, the ongoing process of nationality-formation, too, remained handicapped in Assam as elsewhere in India.

Ever since its beginnings in the early 19th century, our nationalism has been developing at two levels - one all-India, on the basis of pan-Indian cultural homogeneities and an anti-imperialism shared in common; and another, regional (Bengali, Marathi, Asamiya, etc.), on the basis of regional-cultural homogeneities. From the very outset, the two nationalisms are found intertwined and dovetailed. Traditionally, an average Indian identifies himself with both the nationalisms except in some peripheral areas (e.g., Nagaland and Mizoram), left untouched by the railways and by the Indian national movement. Assam is, however, fairly integrated with the rest of India, both economically, culturally and politically. Like an average Indian, an average Asamiya, too, is simultaneously aware of both his regional and Indian identities. Like Shankar Dev, Madhav Dev, a 16th century Vaishnava saint of Assam, wrote in a verse that he was proud of his birth in 'Bharata', and this fact is often invoked as a symbol of the latter identity. Yet another aspect of the development is that, after the British had quit, no particular nationality could be identified as an oppressor nation in relation to other nationalities within the Union, as the Russians could be in the Czarist State.

The duality of our national consciousness found expression in the articulated attitudes of Dhekiyal-Phukan, Bankimchandra Chattopadhyay and M.G. Ranade, and also of the later heirs to their tradition. In his presidential address at the annual conference of the Assam Sahitya Sabha at Dhubri in 1926, Benudhar Rajkhowa (1872-1955), for instance, said:

> 'Let all nationalities (jati) of India follow their own paths. The Brahmaputra, the Ganga, the Yamuna, the Kaveri, the Sindhu - let all of them go on and flow along their respective courses. Let there be no attempts to merge one with the other. Finally, all will converge in the Indian Ocean, that is the Indian nation (mahajati). Troubles will increase if any other method is resorted to for creating the Indian nation (trans. ours)'.

Rajkhowa was happy to note in the course of the same address that a large number of Bengali Muslims from the neighbouring district of Mymensingh had settled in Assam, and he predicted that they would all be proud to call themselves Asamiyas in due course. His prediction came out to be true.

Asamiya little nationalism began to take shape since the 1850s through political mobilization by the Asamiya middle class on the language issue and, later, on the job and land issues as well. It gradually developed as a comprehensive ideology that underwent organized consolidation during the 1920s. Though basically protectionist and defensive till about 1947, Asamiya little nationalism had, by then, assumed also an aggressive tone as well. For example, while presiding over the annual conference of the Asam Sahitya Sabha in 1927, Tarunram Phukan (1877-1939) said:

> We, Asamiyas, are a distinct nationality *(jati)* amongst Indians. Though our language is Sanskrit-based, it is a distinct language. A *rising nationality shows signs of life by way of extending domination over others.* Alas! It is otherwise (with us); we are incapable of self-defence today! We are not only dependent, but even a dependent neighbour is trying to swallow us, taking advantage of our helplessness. Brother Asamiya! Recollect your past glory to have an understanding of the present situation (trans. and emphasis ours).

Seeds of Chauvinism sown by some such speeches were sure to germinate in due course.

However, until about 1947, Asamiya little nationalism was not a cudgel and there were no language or racial riots. As the Asamiya middle class emerged stronger and more ambitious than ever after Sylhet was shaken off its back, its little nationalism started degenerating into chauvinism and minority-baiting. R.P. Vaghaiwalla, as Census Superinten-dent for Assam in 1951, did not fail to take note of this new trend of “aggressive linguistic nationalism”. Riots directed against non-Asamiyas in 1948, 1950, 1960, 1968, 1972 and 1980 in the Brahmaputra Valley bear him out. Large-scale genocides, giving expression to anti-Bengali hatred in particular, began to take place from 1960 onward.

Both at the all-India and regional levels, the emergence of nationalism was a middle class phenomenon. At the top of the society were the foreign capitalists and their allies, the big landlords; and at its bottom, the primary producers - the toiling peasants, artisans and workers. The middle positions were held by Indian industrialists, traders, petty landlords and various sections of the petty bourgeoisie, urban and rural. A middle class wants to project its own interests as the interests of a large group so that the latter could be politically mobilised in the struggle for power. This is how Indian nationalism as well as regional little nationalism originated. The former aimed at consolidating the all-India market and reserving it for Indian middle classes to the exclusion of the foreign domination. The latter was and is interested in developing the regional market as an exclusive preserve of the regional middle class or classes.

Under colonial constraints, Assam failed to develop a viable capitalist class of its own. By now North Indian big bourgeoisie, in collaboration with foreign capital, are well-entrenched in and at the top of Assam's economy, but there is no Asamiya (for that matter even Bengali) big bourgeois to share the market with them. Asamiya business houses that could be ranked as middle bourgeoisie would hardly exceed half a dozen in number. The Asamiya middle class is therefore virtually constituted of small capitalists and other sections of the petty bourgeoisie including professionals and service-holders; many of them are also simultaneously small landlords. They and their Assam-based Bengali rivals (mostly long settled in Assam or sons of the soil in Cachar), operate at the margin of the big capital-dominated economy - in petty industries, petty trade, professions and administrative services. It is these economic circumstances, and not land relations, that largely explain the traditional anti-Bengali edge of Asamiya little nationalism. Problem of land, too, is a relevant issue, which we shall discuss in a following section. The Asamiya middle class believed - and British civil servants encouraged them in the past to do so -that their own people would be turned into a minority in their homeland unless the

Bengali Muslim peasants' incessant influx into the Brahmaputra Valley since about 1905 was checked. This fear complex was built into their ideology and has been constantly harped on since the 1920s. They raised the cry of the Asamiya nationality and their cultural foothold being in danger with a view to mobilizing the peasant masses behind them.

Little nationalism had an idealism of its own too. Local patriots dug up the ancient glory of the land and rediscovered its literature, art and music. They proudly recalled the phoenix - like reappearance of their language after prolonged suppression during 1837-73. Mother language was looked upon as a sacred vehicle of collective self-assertion. They also found it convenient to identify the Bengali as the stumbling block on their way to progress, and they cultivated a sense of grievance against him. The grievance was based, amongst others, on the fact that the Asamiyas were under-represented and Bengalis over-represented in the services and professions in the province. Lachit Phukan, the 17th century hero who defeated the Mughals at the battle of Saraighat in 1671 was projected as the symbol of resistance to immigrating outsiders. All little nationalists were not necessarily chauvinists. There was scope for one to remain a local patriot and an Indian nationalist at the same time.

Local administration by and jobs for the sons of the soil, introduction of Asamiya as the only medium of instruction in all schools, a halt to settlement of wastelands with immigrants for protection of the indigenous peasants' interests and reorganization of the multilingual province into a linguistic one with Asamiya as the official language - these were the demands that sustained Asamiya little nationalism over the decades. In the 1940s when the danger of the province being absorbed into East Pakistan (Group C of Cabinet Mission Plan, 1946) became imminent, the Anti-Grouping agitation, an assertion of faith in both Indian unity and local autonomy, was led by the local Congress and left parties, in defiance of the All-India Congress Committee's contrary stand in favour of the Cabinet Mission's

Grouping Plan. It was largely because of this stiff opposition that the Cabinet Mission Plan failed, and a partition of India and Assam followed. Henceforth, Bengali - speaking populous Sylhet ceased to be a part of Assam.

Jyoti Prasad Agarwala (1903-51) - Congressman, literateur and founder- president of Assam's IPTA movement - showed how local patriotism, Indian nationalism and internationalism could go together. Whatever was -progressive, democratic and legitimate in the demands raised by Asamiya little nationalism did also find a place in the programme the Assam Pradesh Congress Committee stood for. For example, it stood for reorganization of the province on a linguistic basis and was in favour of the line system as a check to uncontrolled immigration in the Brahmaputra Valley. This Committee had its jurisdiction only over the Brahmaputra Valley - the traditional Asamiya homeland - and, later, also Shillong. Bengali-speaking Cachar and Sylhet were, on the other hand, under the jurisdiction of the Bengal Provincial Congress Committee "until 1947. Nevertheless, despite provocations from Asamiya and Bengali chauvinists, the two Committees were, by and large, able to make a common anti-imperialist cause and stand together on the Sylhet question till 1946. The separate platform of Asamiya little nationalism was constituted of the Asam Sahitya Sabha (estd. in 1917), the Asamiya Samrakshinii Sabha (estd. in 1926) and the Asam Jatiya Mahasabha in the 1930s. Generally, it used to attract government servants, client intellectuals and Congress drop-outs. Nilmani Phukan (1880-1978) and Ambikagiri Raychaudhuri (1885-1967) emerged as their dedicated leaders. Bengali loyalists and chauvinists of the Brahmaputra Valley, on the other hand, looked forward to the Assam Domiciled and Settlers' Association (estd in 1935 and renamed Assam Citizens' Association by 1940, but soon defunct) professedly for the defence of the civil and political rights of all persons having their domicile of choice in Assam. Assamese masses paid least attention to these divisive forces and did not allow themselves to be distracted by such influences from their participation in the anti-imperialist national upsurge.

When the Congress and allied left parties were busy fighting imperialism, the Asamiya little nationalist platform went on projecting British civil servants like Bampfylde Fuller, P.R.T. Gordon and C.S. Mullan as saviours of the Asamiya people. Imperialism encouraged regionalism to counter the Congress movement and looked upon its high priests as allies of the Raj. Rai Bahadur S.K. Bhuyan (1894-1964), who did painstaking and path-breaking research to invoke historical and cultural symbols of Asamiya little nationalism, was nominated to the membership of the Gauhati Municipal Board during the Non-Cooperation days, to act as a check upon the Congress bloc therein. Later in the 1940s, he was persuaded to leave his teaching job in the Cotton College with lien to join the National War Front. Other instances of little nationalists' collaborationist role could also be cited.

While many Asamiya tea planters were with the Congress, wealthier and more powerful ones clung to British imperialism and the Asamiya movement. To propagate the cause, Sivaprasad Barua - the biggest Asamiya and Indian tea planter of his times - started in the 1930s Assam's first and short-lived daily newspaper, the *Dainik Batori,* with Nilmoni Phukan as its editor. It was in course of an article published in this news-daily in 1937 that Jnananath Bora, a law teacher, held out the frivolous threat of Assam's secession from India, obviously to blackmail the Congress movement. This happened even before the Muslim League had taken a similar move. Bora's was still a lone voice, not backed by even his own class, not to speak of the peasant masses who were then deeply involved in the Congress and its Ryot Sabha movement.

Later, in the 1940s, the masses continued to respond to the anti-imperialist struggle and gave electoral support to the Congress, rather than to the little nationalist platform. The Congress stood for separation of Sylhet from Assam, but tried to maintain the broadest possible Assamese unity by shelving parochial demands, like the imposition of Asamiya on the unwilling minorities, that might divide the people. It was only after the 1950s that Assam began to shrink in area with every retreat the Congress made before the tide of rising chauvinism. The Asam Sahitya Sabha's recent demand at its Raha session, 1980, for denying the major minorities of their existing privilege of using their own respective mother tongues as the media of instruction in schools even in their own localities has come as a threat, sowing seeds of dissension in Cachar and tribal areas.

In pre-1947 Assamese society then, the Asamiya middle class and peasantry were under greater influence of the ideals of Indian nationalism than of region-based little nationalism. The social base of the latter remained narrow. Neither the Congress nor the Asamiya little nationalists had at that time mentionable influence over the tribal, Muslim and tea garden labour masses. This reflected a certain degree of non-integration within the Assamese society, no doubt. Nevertheless economic, political and social forces of integration were silently at work and, with elimination of many of the colonial constraints, these emerged stronger during the post-Independence period.

However retarded or distorted, some economic development did take place in Assam attracting hundreds and thousands of peasants and workers - a sizeable number of them from neighbouring Bengal - to the farms, mines, plantations and towns during the last one century and a half. As a result, there has been both diversification and interpenetration of social groups. Through the latter process, the Asamiya society has emerged numerically stronger and culturally more enriched. It has to gain more from the continuing process of voluntary integration.

The limited economic development and assimilation that had taken place despite colonial restraints is an indisputable fact today that can no longer be nullified with retrospective effect. The solution of Assam's national question, looked at from a Marxist point of view, therefore, lies not in putting the clock back, but in an emphasis on assimilation and a halt to further immigration for the sake of' 'national peace'.

II

Class/National Characteristics of the Movement

These are some of the roots of chauvinism that is now resurgent and is represented by the Asam Sahitya Sabha, the Asam Jatiyatavadi Dal and the Purbanchaliya Loka Parishad (PLP) - the latter two floated around 1977. The PLP has a wider vision than the Sabha and the Dal, to the extent that its plans and programmes relate to the entire northeast region that consists of seven sister states. The Sabha, Dal and Parishad, these three are the main constituents of the Gana Sangram Parishad-the united front of all Asamiya regional nationalist forces-which has over 1,200 branches in the state. The Asam Sahitya Sabha, alone, has 700 branches of its own. In the 1970s, every annual conference of the Sabha was attended by several lakhs of people. It is a unique institution which, though actively and formally involved in the current movement, also happens to be a UGC-recognised research body. The All Assam Students' Union (AASU) is another important organization which, together with the Asam Sahitya Sabha, spearheaded the 1972 Asamiya language movement, was in the forefront of the second refinery movement of 1970 as well as the food movement of 1966 and is, again, in the forefront of the current agitation. It represents the student power that has added respectability to chauvinism and a spirit of dedication to the cause.

While untangling Assam's tangled national question, Sanjib Baruah brings into focus not the social classes, but such categories as 'ethnicity', demographic imbalance and 'plural society' as the key determinants of "the logic of political power" in the given situation. But this logic, we assume, cannot be autonomous in operation, it requires the mediation of a class or class-in-making in need of that political power. In Baruah's analysis, too, one finds the students and "socio-cultural and literacy bodies" as the mediators in the process through which the mass agitation is fed with myths and perhaps "a false consciousness". But in terms of economic interests whom do these students (AASU) and the socio-cultural and literacy bodies (Asam Sahitya Sabha) represent? Asamiya toiling peasants and workers? No. They represent the Asamiya middle class or classes, as defined by us, constituted of bourgeois-landlord and petty bourgeois elements. In our view and as its chronology is sketched below, the agitation was started by the Asamiya capitalists and gentry through the communication media they control, and the students and other sections of the petty bourgeoisie including sections of peasants were gradually drawn into it. Ethnicity was not a given factor to which politics responded; rather, ethnicity awareness was encouraged and exploited by the upper classes for political ends.

Although the present movement was formally launched by the students in a big way only a year back, its preparations were being made by the Asamiya bourgeoisie since 1978. Hard-pressed by big capital from above and the rising labour and peasant movements from below and, at the same time, being internally divided by caste politics, the Asamiya upper classes are terribly agitated about the economic stagnation. Not being strong and resourceful enough, they are hardly optimistic about pushing out big capital from positions of domination in industries and trade. So they aspire to monopolize what residual is left over, that is, small industries and petty trade as well as professions and services in their state. Their survival, they think, is dependent on three conditions:

(i) elimination of Bengali and other competitors (for instance, at one stage, the AASU demanded even the abolition of all reservations in the matter of jobs and scholarships for scheduled castes and tribes);

(ii) opportunities of intensification of labour exploitation, unhindered by trade unions (for instance, on November 6, 1979, Nibaran Bora publicly gave out his call to smash the 'Bengali-dominated' trade unions and, still earlier, Jatiyatavadi volunteers had helped city bus owners to break the strike of Guwahati city bus workers; and

(iii) unhindered control over the state administration for the creation of bureaucratic capital of which the Asamiya upper classes could be made the major beneficiaries.

The spurt in the left activities since 1977 goaded them to consolidate their forces on the basis of a chauvinist political programme, which alone was deemed effective to nip the threat in the bud.

The cudgel of chauvinism is handy for capitalists and landlords on several considerations. It could be used to cut to size not only Bengali and other non-Asamiya competitors, but also the workers and tenant farmers, a large number of whom are non-Asamiya, by dividing them. Thirdly, by blackmailing the Centre through connivance with clandestine threats of secessionism, more local power could be gained for the Asamiya upper classes. For, the divisible cake was too small now to accommodate new middle-class elements from the neo-Asamiya community, remaining heretofore backward but now forcing their way to it with claims to a share of the spoils.

The bourgeois-landlord chauvinists skilfully used the press and other communication media to create an impression amongst the politically backward sections of the people that the Bengalis, as a community, are opposed to the aspirations of the Asamiyas, that they are all leftists and that all leftists in Assam, are, in general, agents of Bengali expansionism in eastern India. This stand helped the Asamiya middle class to overcome the caste politics oriented to the Ujani Asam Rajya Parishad and the Other Backward Communities (OBC) faction and emerge united out of the chaos that the divided Congress house was. This stand also initially helped the chauvinists to win over to their cause, or at least neutralize, the local Marwari business houses representing traders, tea planters and industrialists, who were themselves victims of a racial hate campaign and riots during 1966-68. This stand misled the backward toilers and caused a division in the trade unions and the liquidation of some of them.

How the initial phase of the agitation developed 'by and large peacefully' with blessings of the press, organized intimidations and jingoist wall writings, how ceaseless protest meetings fed with myths and false statistics since 1978 finally culminated into a mass hysteria and led to large-scale anti-Bengali pogroms in January and May-June of 1980 is interesting to trace from the files of the local press. An obscure piece of research in a departmental journal of the Dibrugarh University, misconstrued to reflect its author's anti-Asamiya attitude, the misbehaviour of a player of the East Bengal Club in a football match at Guwahati, the naming of the conference venue of the P and T Workers' Unions in Cotton College campus as Bhupendra Nagar in honour of late B.N. Ghosh, an eminent trade unionist of all-India stature - all these were turned into controversial and nasty public issues by the chauvinist local press, ostensively to provoke communal ill-feelings and parochialism. Untruths and slanders were spread about the Bengali's role in Assam. Articles in dozens appeared to convince the credulous masses that if the toiling non-Asamiyas were pushed out, their shares of the cake would go to the sons of the soil.

It was as early as in July 1978 that the working committee of the Asam Sahitya Sabha passed a resolution expressing exaggerated concern over the fresh influx of immigrants across the border. The *Dainik Asam* flashed the news with startling headlines and devoted unusually large space to cover it. Doubtful statistics, often emanating from high officials, continued to be poured into publicity to exaggerate the influx and outsiders' domination over Assam's economy, polity and culture. In an editorial article entitled "Nationalism: In Whose Interest?" in its October 1978 issue, the *Sampratik Samayikii,* a progressive Asamiya monthly, viewed the rising chauvinism as an indication that the conspiracy of the national and international vested interests against the growing leftist forces had started yielding its bitter fruits. The editor deplored the complacency and lack of political will on the part of the left to close their ranks and forestall any further worsening of the situation by an alternative programme of left and democratic unity to combat the danger and, at the same time, to voice the frustrations and injured feelings of the Assamese people.

From June 1979 onwards, the press directed its hatred campaign almost exclusively against the so-called "Bangladeshis" - all post-1951 East Pakistan migrants and their progeny, most of whom did not possess readily acceptable documents to prove their Indian citizenship in a no longer permissive setup. The insistence on documents exposed also the pre-1951 Bengali settlers to humiliations of the foreigner-hunt. The campaign was against immigrants from Nepal as well. 'Detect, Disenfranchise and Deport the Foreigners' and 'No Deletion, No Election' were the populist demands that emerged out of the campaign. On June 8, 1979, there was the first-ever 12-hour Assam Bandh called by the AASU to back the demand of foreign nationals' expulsion. On August 26, the All Assam Gana Sangram Parishad was formed. Then followed the unprecedented popular upsurge in the form of mass sit-ins, picketings, satyagrahas, strikes and a mass signature campaign- all these culminating into the 34-hour Assam Bandh on December 3. Meanwhile, printing press owners, as an organized body, had refused to print the electoral rolls for the Parliamentary Election of 1979-80. On December 10, 1979 the movement claimed its first martyr who reportedly died of a CRP (Central Reserve Police) lathi charge on that day. On December 18, lakhs of people took oath to carry on life-long struggle until all foreigners were ousted. The year ended with the observance of a state-wise Non-Co-operation Week, and the new year began with a 58-hour Assam Bandh. On January 3, the movement claimed a second martyr, who had been murdered under mysterious circumstances. Then followed the large-scale genocide in Kamrup. Boycott of the election all over the state excepting Cachar, was complete. Even gazetted officers on election duty mostly refused to cooperate with the government. Oil was refused to the rest of India. Schools and Colleges were closed. During the period from the collapse of the last Lok Sabha to the installation of Indira Gandhi government into power in January 1980, there was virtually no administration in Assam, and the officers were often seen taking their orders from the AASU and the Gana Sangram Parishad.

Over the months, the movement demonstrated that it could mobilize hundreds and thousands of people without disturbing peace or creating violence, if it so wished. This was feasible also because dissident political and linguistic minorities preferred not to come in their way by holding parallel meetings and processions to disapprove of some of their slogans and methods. The minorities were submissive in general. Yet incidents of intimidation, arson and violence continued to mount from August 1979 resulting in an exodus of Bengali and Nepali settlers in trickles. Soon the Government of West Bengal was forced to open two camps in Jalpaiguri district to accommodate them. Swelling to ten thousand souls by now, they are mostly evicted peasants, tenant farmers, artisans and fishermen. Nepali refugees of Assam origin who found their way to Kathmandu are graziers and peasants and/or retired army men.

The People's Union of Civil Liberties, New Delhi, constituted a fact-finding committee with G.P. Desphpande, Dhirendra Sarma and Chamanlal of the Jawaharlal Nehru University on the Assam Unrest *(Mainstream,* March 8, 1980). After their week-long investigations in Assam during February 9-16, 1980, they submitted a report which is revealing. Between August 1979 and 16 February, altogether 23 persons got killed in Dibrugarh district alone; of them 6 including 4 claimed as martyrs died of police firing and 17 were killed by mob violence or unknown assailants. Of the latter 17, one was an Asamiya and the rest non-Asamiyas, mostly Bengalis as the names suggest. The Committee submitted a long list of persons known to have been killed in other districts as well, but could not make it exhaustive.

The January genocide in North Kamrup alone caused death of some two hundred persons, according to some non-official estimates; dead bodies of only some 80 persons, however, could be found and identified and all of them, excepting two including a non-Asamiya CRP jawan belonged to linguistic or religious minorities. Nearly twenty-five thousand people were rendered homeless by large-scale arson. Retaliatory killings and arsons in Lower Assam, particularly in Nowgong, for days together in the wake of the observance of the Assam Minority Students'

Union's Protest Day on 26 May 1980 far surpassed even what had happened in North Kamrup. As *The Assam Tribune* reported, on the eve of this protest day the president of the AASU had asked the people to 'crush' the counter-agitation. More than three lakhs of minority people had come out on the streets of Lower Assam in protest despite the threat in this context.

The Assam Armed Police acted in a partisan manner and, on one spot at Bijni alone, mowed down at least 23 persons including children on a single day, thus surpassing the earlier record of killing four participants of the anti-foreigner movement of Duliajan on January 18. According to some non-official estimates, the number of deaths due to violence, directly and indirectly connected with the year-old movement so far is a thousand or so. The butchering of minorities went under-reported and mostly unlamented in the local bourgeois press and on the platform of the movement.

There has been premature and even late attempts at making the CPI (M) and a certain statement of Jyoti Basu in November 1979 the scapegoat for all that happened in Assam. What was that statement? It expressed nothing but goodwill for the Assamese people and concern about what would happen if the West Bengal-bound exodus were to attain serious proportions. Even *The Assam Tribune,* November 8, 1979, otherwise rabidly partisan to the movement, found it innocent and published the news along with a gist of Basu's view under the following caption: "Fear of Assamese about Outsiders Is Genuine and Real - Says Jyoti Basu". In course of its resolution dated September 21 and a note submitted to the Government-sponsored all-party meeting at Delhi on November 28, 1980, the Assam State Committee of the CPI (M) called for an immediate sealing off of the Bangladesh border to stop infiltration and start detecting and deporting the real foreigners, in accordance with the country's law and international agreements. The CPI and other left parties, too, had taken a similar stand on the foreigner issue. But all these parties insisted, at the same time, on the due process of law so that citizens of the minority communities were not harassed in the wake of the foreigner-hunt. They were all aware that the so-called 1951 national register of citizens was not admissible as a proof of one's citizenship under the Indian Evidence Act, as had been noted in a judgment of the Gauhati High Court. This conditional and limited support to the cause was interpreted as half-hearted, even mischievous, and violent attacks were concentrated on the left in general and the CPI (M) in particular. So far, five CPI and two CPI (M) cadres - the latter on July *2,* 1980 - have been killed by fanatics let loose by the movement. On August 17, the press in which the Asamiya progressive weekly, *Kalakhar,* is printed was attacked and damaged, and a students' and youth rally, opposed to the movement, at Guwahati was broken up by force. These are only select instances of the reign of terror. Hundreds of leftist cadres have been beaten up, tortured and maimed, expelled from their villages or are under social boycott. They are facing all these brutalities with exemplary heroism, to defend the principles of a consistent democracy. In July and August seven all-India parties jointly held a series of successful public meetings in select towns of Assam, as had been carefully planned, to assert their freedom of expression and movement. This provoked the AASU president to come out with a public threat that they will no longer be "allowed" to carry on their counter-agitation.

Table 6.2: Distribution of Scheduled Tribe Population of Assam

	No. in Thousands		Growth	Decadal %age Growth
	1961	1971		1961-71
Brahmaputra Valley	943	1,329	386	40.9
Autonomous Hills Area	211	263	52	24.6
Cachar	14	15	1	7.1
State of Assam	1,168	1,607	439	37.5

Note: The enumeration is tribe-wise, not language-wise.
Source: Processed from relevant census data in *Statistical Handbook,* Assam, Gauhati, Annual Series.

What is the character of the movement then? Although it has the appearance of an Asamiya national movement, its content is undemocratic and rabidly anti-left. Its methods are double-faced' and proto-fascist. The destructive anger it roused, has been directed not against bourgeois and landlord properties, but the thatched huts and liberty of a section of the poor people and the dissidents. Aspirations of the Asamiya middle class are well-articulated in course of the agitation and propaganda, but not the anti-feudal demands of the peasantry. Another noticeable feature of the movement is a tendency to disown the humanist liberal and intellectual elements in the national heritage of Asamiya culture with a view to revive its clerical, conservative aspects. Thoughts of Jyotiprasad Agarwala and Bishnu Rabha are being misconstrued, divested of some of their humanist liberal content and misused for the purposes of the movement. (Both Agarwala and Rabha were, incidentally, progressive and internationalist in outlook; the former died as a close friend and the latter as an active leader of the communist movement in Assam). Hence, despite mass participation, the middle class character of the movement cannot be denied. More about this in a following section.

Table 6.3: 1971 Population, Assam-Mizoram
(Birth Place Data on the Basis of 1 Per Cent Sample)

Born in	*Number (Thousand)*	*Percentage to Total Population*
Assam and Mizoram	13213	88.4
Other Indian States	701	4.7
Pakistan	931	6.2
Nepal	92	0.6
Other foreign countries	6	0.1
Total population	14943	100

Source : G.K. Mehrotra, "Birth Place Migration in India", *Census of India* 1971, Special Monograph No. *I,* New Delhi, 1974, Appendix B, pp. 15-19.

III

Bengali Influx and Fear Psychosis

Who are the foreigners? In 1978 and early 1979, the terms *"bideshi"* (foreigner) and *"bahiragata"* (outsider) were used interchangeably. These terms not only covered non-Indians, but also those from India's other states. Later, the Asam Sahitya Sabha-the intellectual wing and senior-most constituent of the Gana Sangram Parishad - intervened to narrow down the meaning of the term to post-1951 immigrants from foreign countries with questionable citizenship status, and this got wide acceptance amongst the other constituents of the movement. It represented a major tactical shift.

The AASU and the Gana Sangram Parishad estimate the number of such foreigners at 45 lakhs, almost all of them of Bengali stock. This means that the AASU and the GSP want nearly one-fourth of Assam's present estimated population of 188 lakhs to be declared stateless and removed. They are mostly toiling peasants, artisans and workers, born or residing in the state for a period up to 30 years, virtually as naturalized citizens. They were given shelter and relief, and in many cases even wastelands by the government. Besides, patronage and hospitality were also extended to them by their Asamiya neighbours, so that they could make Assam their new home.

Being poor and illiterate and because of constant mobility in search of a living and in the wake of recurrent race riots, most settlers lost their 'border slips', refugee camp cards and even refugee registration certificates. They failed to take advantage of the constitutional provisions for their naturalization because of these reasons and general indolence. For their failure, the bureaucracy is also to be blamed. For it did not provide easy and inexpensive access to such a validation procedure. Whatever be their formal status now, these settlers are, in any case, already assimilated or are on the way to assimilation.

That there has been large-scale immigration of Bengalis to Assam, mainly from Sylhet - once part of Assam - and East

Bengal during the last seven decades and that the state's population has been growing at an alarming decadal rate of 35 per cent since 1951 are well-known facts*. But what is not noted generally is that more than four-fifths of the decadal population growth is due to natural growth and only about one-fifth or so due to immigration. Space does not permit us to elaborate the basis of our estimate here, except for one exercise.

Let us take the indigenous tribes listed for the Brahmaputra Valley who constitute 11 per cent of its population. These listed tribes are Bodo/Bodokachari, Mech, Hojai, Kachari/Sonowal, Tiwa (Lalung), Rabha, Deuri and Mishing (Miri), whose number outside the valley is insignificant. In fact, they are conspicuously absent in Bangladesh or any other foreign country. The tribal population under scrutiny is visibly almost free of any migration-induced demographic change. Yet the rate of population growth for this tribal group for the decade 1961-71 is as high as 41 per cent as against a 38 per cent growth for the Brahmaputra Valley population as a whole (Table 2). Even with a reasonable margin of error allowed, the tribal case surely demonstrates a very high rate of natural growth in Assam. This is due to a high birth rate and lowered death rate resulting from public health measures. This cuts to size the exaggerated role ascribed to migration in Assam's population growth in recent times and corroborates S.K. Dass's contrary findings in *EPW,* (May 10, 1980).

The immigration into Assam, we are told by Sanjib Baruah, is "on a scale that has few parallels anywhere in the world within a relatively short period". Had he done a little homework, he would have found a parallel in some other parts of India as well at least in neighbouring West Bengal. According to the birth-place data of the Census of India, migrants from outside the state constituted 15.7 per cent of the population of West Bengal in 1961 and 11.9 per cent in 1971. The comparable figures for Assam are 11.4 and 10.2 per cent, respectively - thus in both the years lower than in West Bengal. What is to be noted is the declining trend in both cases. The absence of migration-induced social tension in West Bengal, despite a sizeable number of the migrants and despite a majority of the industrial workers in its organized sector continuing to be non-Bengalis, is also a fact to be noted. West Bengal's position slided down from the first to the third amongst India's states in the scale of industrialization during the post-Independence years, thus, bringing in its trail mounting unemployment, economic discontent and a fertile soil for Bengali chauvinism to strike its roots in the agonies of West Bengal.

The exact number of post-1951 settlers in Assam, together with their locally born progeny, is and will remain an unknown quantity. Yet fair estimates are not impossible. Birth place data for Assam including Mizoram indicate separately the number of residents born outside the states (Table 3) along with information on duration of residence in the state of enumeration. From these data, we could get the number of actual migrants who entered Assam from foreign countries during 1951-61 and 1961-71. But such data do not cover the children born of them in Assam. Again, the language data cover all, but do not distinguish between the post-1951 and old settlers (Table 1). Nor do these data include those migrants who have meanwhile changed their language for Asamiya. Nevertheless, these two sets of data, together with the available periodic counts of registered displaced persons, might make a fair estimate possible if the task is left to the research staff of the Registrar General of Census Operations. It appears, as per our quick estimates, that the number of post-1951 settlers with questionable citizenship status would in no case exceed 13 lakhs by any measure and that the number of persons born in Pakistan (including Bangladesh) and enumerated in Assam shows a declining trend over the period 1951-1971. Of these 13 lakhs, less than 3 lakhs appear to be post-1971 settlers.

No doubt there is a fear psychosis, built into the Asamiya mind, of being outnumbered by outsiders in due course. This fear had an objective basis too, during the British period, as I had elaborately shown in my book, *Planter-Raj to Swaraj,* in 1977. During that period the Asamiya population, numbering less than 7 to 8 lakhs around 1826 and 15 lakhs in 1901, was growing very slowly, both in absolute and relative terms and their language was under many handicaps, was even suppressed for long 36 years, 1837-1873. But the situation radically changed since Independence, with an ascendant Asamiya middle class. From 20 lakhs in 1931, the number of Asamiya speakers in Assam leaped to 50 lakhs in 1951 and to 89 lakhs by 1971. Asamiya poetry, fiction, literary criticism and music are now at a height that was never attained at any point of time during the post-Shankardeva period till our Independence.

In the province/state of Assam, the share of the Asamiya linguistic community in the total population moved up from 23 per cent in 1931 to 55 per cent in 1951, 57 per cent in 1961 and 61 per cent in 1971. If we keep in view only die area that constitutes Assam today, then the share has increased from 36 per cent in 1931, to 62 per cent in 1951 and to 61 per cent in 1971.

The Bengali-speaking population, on the other hand, has been growing more modestly with its share in the total population of reconstituted Assam of today, steadily declining from 30 per cent in 1931 to 21 per cent in 1951 and 20 per cent in 1971. During the 1951-71 period, the state's Bengali linguistic group expanded only 71 per cent, while the Asamiya linguistic group expanded 80 per cent.

In consequence of these changes, Asamiya achieved the status of official language of the state in 1961. It is also, together with English, the sole medium of instruction at the level of University education since 1972. These are welcome developments which, after some conflicts, were accepted by the linguistic minorities on a give and take basis. Thus, the exceptionally high demographic growth, due to both natural growth as well as linguistic conversion, provided an expanded base to the Asamiya middle class for the exercise of state-wise cultural and political domination within reasonable limits.

The above analysis, relevant to the last half-century and based on Census data, shows that the population influx in general, and the Bengali influx in particular, has not created any linguistic imbalance in Assam, which could be deemed as detrimental to the Asamiya cause. Neither has it disturbed the religious balance over the period 1941-1971. In the reconstituted Assam of today, the proportion of the Muslims to the total population remained almost static - near about 25 per cent throughout this period. In fact, between 1951 and 1971 this share decreased from 24.7 per cent to 24.6 per cent. For, while the state's Hindu population increased 83.4 per cent and the Sikh and Jain communities at a much faster rate meanwhile, the comparable growth for the Muslims was only 81.2 per cent. Thus, whether judged in terms of the balance between the major linguistic communities or between the major religious communities, the pre-1951 situation remained virtually the same also in 1971. The theory of the Asamiya language and culture being in danger today is, therefore, more a myth than a reality.

The influx into Assam is surely the central focus of the recent movement and social tension. However, while discussing this Sanjib Baruah introduces a number of misleading half-truths. He says, for instance, "Origins of immigration into Assam began at the turn of the century when Assam's virgin lands were opened up for East Bengal refugees". In fact, rural immigration started in the wake of the tea industry half a century earlier and attained a , much larger scale after big tracts of virgin lands were made over to the tea planters. Tea garden labour immigration and their settlement on wasteland in the Brahmaputra Valley continued on a big scale with intermittent vigour, right up to the 1930s. Nearly 15 lakh acres of government lands were directly settled with the foreign tea planters, as their private properties by 1940-41. On the other hand, another 11 lakh acres of government lands were settled with various groups of migrants from other provinces including ex-garden labour for ordinary cultivation; of this, only 5 lakh acres, with migrants from East Bengal (relevant annual report of the Land Revenue Department, Government of Assam).

Baruah's description of a "sudden demographic change" is also a historical. There was no question of "emergence" of a plural society either; that too, suddenly. For, the plurality and the integrative process are twin phenomena of the Assamese society (as much as of the Indian society at large) that have been continuing for many centuries. Assam was not free of immigration and plurality in any period of history. Indo-Aryan and Mongoloid elements continually came into the population-poor valley and intermingled to form the Asamiya/ Assamese society. Any further influx may be unwelcome now on grounds, economic and political, but facts need not be given a twist to suit one's theory of culture being in a crisis.

After having said this about the fear psychosis and its basis, let us now examine the *modus operandi* of the chauvinists to sustain the fear, even when its objective basis is somewhat thin in the post-Independence period. We shall limit out citations to only recent propaganda carried on by the Asam Sahitya Sabha - a major constituent and ideological inspirer of the movement. It is claimed that the movement is above racism and is not directed against the Bengali community as such. Yet, in its printed Memorandum submitted to the President of India on November 4, 1979, which is widely circulated, it makes "Bengali Hindus", as a community, responsible for the suppression of the Asamiya language in the schools and courts of Assam in 1836. In its Memorandum submitted to the Home Minister on February 23,1980, also printed and widely circulated, the same charge is repeated:

> There were Bengali-speaking people and *on their advice* Bengali was introduced in the courts of justice and other government offices and schools in Assam (emphasis ours).

The statement was not necessary at all to boost a movement professedly directed against the foreigners only, nor is there any historical truth in it. The East India Company did not rule and formulate its policies according to the advice of its 'native' clerks.

The research of Benudhar Sarma (b 1894), a distinguished historian and life-long associate of the Sabha, had decisively blasted the myth in an article in *Pravandha-Saurabh* (in Asamiya) long back, quoting Francis Jenkins who as Commissioner had taken the decision. He wrote: "It was I who was at the root of the advice in favour of introducing Bengali. I was in favour of Bengali. It was my orders that Robinson carried out" (retranslated). The fact that many Bengalis like Ramlochan Sen, Janakinath Sen, Swarupchandra Dewan, Madanmohan Ghosh Dewan and no less a personality than R.C. Dutt lent active support to the cause of the restoration of the status of Asamiya by 1873 and that dozens of Bengalis starting with Jaychandra Chakravarty, Abhayshankar Guha, Gopalkrishna De and Rajmohan Nath were involved in the Asamiya literary movement even in its most critical days are also known to the Sabha. Ashutosh Mukherjee and P.C. Ray successfully fought Bengali chauvinism in defence of the rights of the Asamiya language. Yet the Asam Sahitya Sabha goes on repeating an untruth, with obviously understandable purposes.

This is but one instance of how the mass frenzy is created and directed against the Bengalis. The Sabha's reaction to the North Kamrup genocide - the bitter fruit of the frenzy it nurtured - is also worth noting. In "Eclipse of the East: An Analysis of the Present Agitation in Assam" (Asam Sahitya Sabha, 1980), p 2, it is observed: "The recent outbreaks of violence resulting in Assamese villages of North Kamrup becoming refugees in their own state, the arson and looting of Assamese villages, the rape of Assamese village women and the brutal murder of a CRP jawan bear testimony to the militant posture and expansionist design of Bangladeshi immigrants in Assam." Fed by such Goebbles-like propaganda, the Asamiya patriotic masses really came to believe that they, and not their Bengali and neo-Asamiya neighbours, were the victims of the genocide.

As has been noted by many, fantastically exaggerated statistics raising the number of foreigners from an initial 13 lakh to 45 and even to 51 or 70 lakhs, also contributed to the frenzy. Languagewise, Bengalis and Nepalis in Assam numbered only 29 lakhs and 3.5 lakhs, respectively, in 1971. As per birth-place data, there were no more than 10 lakhs of persons born in foreign countries, mostly in Pakistan (Bangladesh), in the same year. It is hence clear that the target, set by the anti-foreigner movement far in excess of the population of either category, was to deliberately mislead the people so that they reacted with a do-or-die spirit. On the other hand, these exaggerated figures made the minorities apprehensive of attacks on their own citizenship rights as well. This is one of the reasons why the social base of the movement later became narrower than what it initially was. People's demand that Assam should not be burdened with further immigration from foreign lands and that all *genuine* foreigners, who do not substantively qualify for citizenship in terms of law and Constitution, should be detected and removed is legitimate. It was accepted in principle by the Central government and all major Indian political parties by September 1979 and, this acceptance they reiterated again and again. Yet the dispute lingers on because the movement refuses to admit even those immigrants who have stayed for ten years or more in India or are born in India - and whose parents or grandparents were born in undivided India - thus substantively qualifying themselves for naturalized citizenship as provided for by our Constitution. The movement's insistence on the so-called 1951 National Register of Citizens as the basic document for determining citizenship is motivated by this refusal.

NATIONAL REGISTER OF CITIZENS, 1951

If 1951 is accepted as the cut-off year, then several lakhs of families will have to be asked to pack up and go, after they had resided in Assam for up to 30 years, reared their children and grandchildren here and largely assimilated themselves to the original people in many ways. The cruelty of asking people to undergo the sufferings of an Operation Deportation after a generation gap apart, one may perhaps pertinently question its practicability. Is it feasible at all, short of a civil war or gendarme-backed fascist terror?

Even if feasible and even if the 1951 Register is finally dug up out of oblivion, one may still have doubts about the legality of its use for the purpose. The Prefatory Note of Vol XII, Census of India 1951, Part I-B, relevant to Assam, Tripura and Manipur, informs us that as a part of census work.

> .... there are National Registers of Citizens, prepared simultaneously with the filing up of enumeration slips, giving important details for each person of every village or ward in a town. These Registers are preserved in manuscript as permanent records in District offices.

But under section 15 of the Census Act, records prepared by the Census officers are neither open to inspection nor admissible in evidence in any legal proceeding. In a test case of 1967, the Gauhati High Court refused to consider the copy of an entry in NRC, 1951 as an admissible proof of one's citizenship *(AIR* 1970, Assam and Nagaland 206) precisely on the above grounds, *inter alia.* This explains why the Government of India, while having allowed the police intelligence to consult it in their search for foreigners in the 1960s, is hesitant now to admit this publicly and to commit that the practice would continue. If the NRC is not a public document according to the Census Act, how could it be made available to a citizen to establish his claim? Or, how could it be mended if, e.g., one's name is not entered by mistake?

In any case, we have shown above, no basic inter-community imbalance was created during the period 1951-71 that might be said to have threatened Asamiya culture in its religious and linguistic aspects. Under the circumstances, 1971 should have been accepted as the cut-off year by the movement, had the fear of being swamped been the real and major concern. It needs to be stressed that even if all those who came to Assam till March 25, 1971 (birth-date of Bangladesh) are absorbed, the state's cultural map remains almost the same as it was in 1951. Why not then think in terms of expelling only the post-1971 infiltrators, the sealing off of the border and other safeguards rather than putting the clock back?

IV

Self-Determination or Self-Annihilation

"The principle of nationality is historically inevitable in bourgeois society and taking this society in due account", said Lenin in 1913, "the Marxist fully recognizes the historical legitimacy of national movements". Yet, in continuation of his argument, he also warned:

> But to prevent this recognition from becoming an apologia of nationalism, it must be strictly limited to what is progressive in such movements, in order that this recognition may not lead to bourgeois ideology obscuring proletarian consciousness *(Collected Works,* Vol 20, Moscow, 1964, p. 34).

These guidelines hold good for Marxists of any country when they face the national question at the stage of the democratic revolution. Let us see how Gail Omvedt applies her Marxism to the Assam situation.

Almost the sole demand of the year-old movement is the expulsion of all those whom it considers as foreigners, with reference to the NRC, 1951. Its reluctance to thrash out all other pressing demands, even the economic ones until then leaves no ambiguity about this prime objective. The movement is built up on the false belief that such foreigners constitute about one-fourth of Assam's population. Surely amongst them there are some landlords, capitalists and other exploiters just as there are among the Asamiyas and among people of all nationalities. But that does not justify the movement's untiring and indiscriminate tirades against all of them.

We have shown that neither the overall linguistic nor the religious balance, in terms of proportions internal to the Assamese society, has been affected by the migration movements of 1951-71. This may not be convincing for Gail Omvedt. She might still argue that since Asamiya national culture is threatened by changes in its original racial base, this makes an Operation Deportation all the more necessary to preserve that base and restore the 1952 voting potential to the people so that their autonomy and homeland were not robbed of their original racial content. Omvedt does not mind even if that means rendering lakhs of settled peasants and workers homeless and economically ruined. But for Marxists, and even for liberal democrats, such a solution is monstrous and questionable.

Does history furnish us with other examples of this kind of negative demand - and on such a scale - being equated with the urge for "self-determination"? Two such examples come off-hand to our mind. In Germany, the National Socialist Party's demand for disenfranchisement and deportation of the Jews in the name of the purification and unification of the German nation led ultimately to disastrous consequences for them as well as others. Again, in Pakistan, the Muslim League's insistence on treating the non-Muslims on a separate footing as "jimmis" and on an exchange of population with India - all this in the name of self-determination of the Pakistanis - only helped disintegrate Pakistan itself and strengthen the forces of authoritarianism and subsequent army rule.

One finds yet a third example from the history of Assam itself. During the second half of the 18th century, the Ahom Court did carry out a determined struggle to identify and wipe out the Mayamarias (a protestant religious sect representing the whole Moran tribe and others), then estimated to be 8 lakhs or about one-third of the Assamese population, in the name of protecting cows, brahmans and culture. The result was a lingering civil war for three decades and total ruin of Assam, its population coming down to just half of what it was and its smiling fields turned into sprawling wastelands, Much of the stagnation in Assam's peasant economy during the 19th century may be traced back to that calamity. Assam's anti-foreigner movement, unless self-restrained in time, might also lead to disintegration not only of the Assamese but also of the Indian society, which is a mosaic of ethnic diversities. The January and May-June anti-Bengali pogroms and their subsequent impact on the agrarian economy of Lower Assam are pointers.

Omvedt's "Loss of territory" (not of peasant-occupied lands, but mostly wastelands "lost" to equally exploited migrant peasants and artisans) argument to explain the anti-foreigner movement in terms of defence of national self-determination is not convincing. These migrants did not come as conquerors and exploiters but as sources of cheap labour supply to not only the big bourgeoisie, but also to the Asamiya landlords and the rising Asamiya capitalists. If this combination had broken down-as Omvedt says - the outdated modes of cultivation of the autochthons, is that a sufficient reason to put the clock back by three decades to get rid of them and the process?[1] Are not these mostly independent immigrants, small peasants, agricultural workers and tenants, and not landlords, in relation to their Asamiya neighbours? If so, the Asamiya nationalism connected with such land relations is gentry nationalism, not peasant nationalism. The original settlers may be dead, but catch hold of their children and grand-children and deport, even if they were horn in Assam and are toilers! Such is the solution from a professed disciple of Lenin!

Let us see what Lenin had to say in a somewhat similar context. The historically-rooted mistrust between the Little and Great Russians in 1913 was no less than what prevails today between the Asamiyas and the Bengalis, but more because the Russians were an oppressor nation, dominating every sphere of the Czarist State, economic, cultural and political. Yet, while making a note of the old modes being broken down by the migrants in Ukraine, Lenin observed:

For several decades a well-defined process of accelerated economic development has been going on in the South, i.e., the Ukraine, attracting hundreds of thousands of peasants and workers from Great Russia to the capitalist farms, mines and cities. The 'assimilation' - within these limits - of the Great Russian and Ukrainian proletariat is an indisputable fact. And this fact is *undoubtedly* progressive. Capitalism is replacing the ignorant, conservative settled muzhik of the Great Russian and Ukrainian backwoods with a mobile proletarian whose conditions of life break down specifically narrow-mindedness, both Great Russian and Ukrainian. *(Collected Works,* Vol 20, p. 31).

All this Lenin said despite the fact that Russia and Ukraine were unequal partners locked in an oppressor-oppressed relationship. To drive home the point to fellow Marxists, he continued:

> Even if we assume that, in time, there will be a state frontier between Great Russia and the Ukraine, the historically progressive nature of the 'assimilation' of the Great Russian and Ukrainian will be as undoubted as the progressive nature of the grinding down of nations in America *(ibid}*.

Later in 1919 Lenin saw that the Ukrainian language was given due status and more Ukrainians got government jobs in their own state, but never did he advise deportation of Russians from the Ukrainian soil.

Omvedt's use of the term "self-determination" in the Assam context is also inappropriate as a Marxist proposition. Lenin made it clear in course of his many writings that the multinational centralized states were a tremendous historical step forward from medieval disunity, and therefore, Marxists were opposed to their disintegration. What was necessary, according to Lenin to ensure 'consistent democracy' and elimination of national oppression in such states, was to follow the Swiss model and to create autonomous areas, however small, with homogeneous populations, as far as practicable to which "members of the respective nationalities scattered all over the country ...could gravitate". Marxists demand not a right to autonomy but straightway autonomy itself. For, it is an integral aspect of consistent democracy they stand for. Self-determination, on the other hand, is more than autonomy; it is the right to secede and form a separate state. Marxists do not popularize the demand for self-determination on their own, but only recognize the right to it, "where such a movement is actually in existence" and is directed against an oppressor nation which is economically and culturally dominant within the State. Again even where this right is recognized, the decision of the relevant working class might be in favour of opposing secession, depending upon the national and international circumstances. *(Collected Works,* Vol 20, pp. 45-6, 405, 410, 441 and Vol 22, p. 345.)

It is in consideration of these basic principles that Omvedt should have refrained from her childish prattle over self-determination when such a demand (in the Marxist sense) has not been on the agenda of the movement itself. Although the idea is toyed with by peripheral forces therein, it has not yet emerged as a class demand. Even if it does, a true Marxist will oppose it and continue to demand more of autonomy and equality for all nationalities and languages, big and small in a united India - if necessary through a revision of the Centre-state relations in favour of the latter and creation of new autonomous areas for tribal populations within the constituent states. Encouragement to divisive forces and disruption of the unity of working people will lead the people of Assam not to self-determination but to self-annihilation. Assam can defeat the rule of Indian big bourgeoisie only in close co-operation with the working people of all Indian nationalities. Let us therefore emphasize 'assimilation' as an alternative solution of the problem. Lenin said in this context:

> Fight for every kind of national development, for 'national culture' in general? Of course, not. The economic development of capitalist society presents us with examples of immature national movements . . . and also examples of assimilation of nations. The proletariat, however, far from undertaking to uphold the national development of every nation, on the contrary, warns the masses against such illusions, stands for the fullest freedom of capitalist intercourse and welcomes every kind of assimilation of nations, except that which is founded on force or privilege *(Collected Works,* Vol. 20, p. 35).

For more than the past one hundred years, large-scale immigration has been said to be a threat to the Asamiya society and culture. Yet, like Pisa's leaning tower, it still maintains its tall existence and even grows at a rate faster than in the case of any other linguistic group in India and casting its shadow over the tribal and other minority groups. Its numerical dominance as a linguistic community in the state, as a ratio to the total population, is also higher today than in any past period. How did this miracle happen? Along the path of assimilation, an age-old, active historical process. During the pre-British period, the Asamiya society swelled its ranks by absorbing autochthonous tribal groups as well as Tai-Ahom and north-Indian immigrants. This process continued through the British period and reached out to the immigrating tea labour, Nepali and Bengali communities. The trend i.e. assimilation, is expected to continue unless halted and reversed by repeated anti-minority pogroms and a reaction thereto.

Given the high rate of linguistic assimilation, we repeat, the fear of the Asamiyas being swamped by Bengalis has little objective basis. This fear was cultivated by British civil servants like Gordon and Mullan in the past, as was pointed out earlier as a part of their divide and rule policy. Under the Raj, political participation through separate electorates, settlement of wastelands in communal and caste blocs under the Line System and segregated schools and syllabi for the majority and minority communities - these were some of the features of this divide and rule policy. Mullan, in his 1931 Census Report, provocatively described the immigration process as an 'invasion' and 'conquest' and predicted that Sibsagar would ultimately remain the only Asamiya home district. His prediction has not come out to be true. Nor was his interpretation of the census data held correct. The Governor of Assam had to clarify and tell the Assam Legislative Council in 1933 that, despite heavy immigration since 1901, the percentage of speakers of Asamiya to total population had remained "very steady" and that "the language at present is in no danger of suppression" (ALC Proc, 1933, Vol 13, p. 5). If it was true of 1931, it is much more so today since the ratio of Asamiya-speakers to total population has increased enormously meanwhile both in the Brahmaputra Valley and the state of Assam as a whole. This is the result of assimilation.

Sanjib Baruah's obsession with Myron Weiner and the "concept of plural society" (not the Laskian, but its neo-colonialist variant meant for the consumption of third world scholarship) leads to his skepticism about assimilation. What has developed, in Assam, notes Baruah, is "not a composite society of peoples who mingle with one another, but a plural society of separate communities", and that politicians "had hardly contributed to a genuine integration of the communities and evolution of composite cultural patterns". Such platitudinous statements could be made to describe any nationality in making, the United States in its formative stage and China not excluded. In the former, ethnicity-oriented voting blocs are still an important aspect of the political culture.

The process of nationality-formation does initially exhibit inter-group tensions. Yet, given appropriate leadership and time - as was seen in the days of *Ujani-Namani* (Upper Assam and Lower Assam) conflicts - the formative process goes ahead overcoming the specific contradictions among the people. The social scientist should also concern himself with 'what is becoming', instead of being solely occupied with 'what is'. A plural situation is not something static and insurmountable, but is correlated with the pace of economic development. It is the economy, not society or polity, that one should primarily look into for the roots of the malady for a cure. This does not mean that ethnicity and politics are of no importance and the national question can be untangled through the economic measures alone. As Lenin pointed out long back, that would be sheer economism.

To say that there has been no real assimilation in Assamese society is as much a half-truth as saying that assimilation is complete. Available census data on the mother tongue and bilinguism leave no doubt about the fact of assimilation, though much remains to be achieved. During 1931-71, the number of Asamiya-speakers made a great leap forward from 20 to 89 lakhs and their percentage proportion to the state population from 36 per cent (adjusted for reorganization of the state and made comparable) to 61 per cent. But Baruah is not happy with this growth since "the Bengali Muslims" who had *en masse* returned Asamiya as their mother tongue consistently for the last three censuses as a matter of "political act", might shift their language loyalty and join the "urban Bengali Hindus" to spite the real Asamiyas! The contrary RSS propaganda has been that they are in league with the Asamiya Muslims to spite the Asamiya and Bengali Hindus! Such is the logic of the ethnicity approach to politics.

The decision of Bengali Muslim settlers of the Brahmaputra Valley to eschew the League politics, support the Congress and merge their linguistic identity with the major language and culture was indeed a political act in 3948 with a view to minimizing social tension. It was also an act of political wisdom-an expression of genuine urge for assimilation comparable to, say, the voluntary integration of diverse migrant groups to the dominant linguistic group in the US. Wrote the Census Superintendent of Assam in 1961: "When they come to Assam, those Muslim immigrants honestly try to know the Assamese language and send their children to schools where the Assamese language is the medium of instruction". They have been intermarrying with Asamiya Muslims. They have been long adopted by their Asamiya neighbours as Neo-Asamiyas. Even Nilomoni Phukan, one of the high priests of little nationalism, said in 1972:

> Today these very immigrants, having undergone assimilation to the Asamiya society have been able to take their rightful place in the realm of language and culture and, with equal access to leadership, have been able to share the responsibility of the country's administration on an equal footing. This is the normal path to naturalization (D. Chaudhuri, *Nilamani Phukanar Chintadhara,* Guwahati, 1972, p. 91, trans ours).

It is a pity that Baruah does not share this optimism and wisdom and, instead, is in constant dread of a sinister world of pretensions all around. Despite possible drifts in language loyalties at the margin and lags between a formal change of language and firm emotional and cultural integration, the overall long-term trend is unmistakably set by the last three censuses, in favour of Asamiyaisation.

From their second generation, the Bengali migrants' major dialect, Mymensinghia, began to borrow words and even idioms from their Asamiya neighbours. As a result, by now, their dialect - like Sadri or Garden-baat spoken in tea gardens and ex-garden labour villages - is increasingly gravitating to Asamiya. For it has once for all lost its anchorage in distant East Bengal. Thus, Sadri and Mymensinghia might be accepted as newly developed dialects of the Asamiya language. Indeed, the Asam Sahitya Sabha did a good job by getting folk tales in the latter dialect collected and published. Assimilation is facilitated also by the awareness that Bengali and Asamiya have a sizeable common vocabulary and a common script, with the exception of only two letters in the alphabet.

Rural Bengali Hindus also tend to follow their Muslim brethren in respect of opting for linguistic assimilation. Many such people were victims of recent riots in North Kamrup, amongst whom were people who had even adopted typically Asamiya surnames to be more acceptable to the society at large. All these people used to send their children to Asamiya-medium schools and spoke flawless local dialect. Thus, linguistic assimilation involves both Bengali Muslims and Bengali Hindus, though with a varying degree. The trend is reflected also in contemporary Asamiya literature. Sakina Khatun, Ilimuddin Dewan, Rajmohan Nath, Dhiren Datta and Rabindra Sarkar - these are some of the neo-Asamiya writers of Bengali stock, who have contributed to Asamiya literature. Sananta Tanti, a son of the tea garden soil of Cachar, has added to contemporary Asamiya poetry a new vigour that emerges from the rural proletariat.

The Tai-Ahoms took at least three to four centuries to completely Asamiyaise themselves by the 17th century. But some of the recently Asamiya communities have not taken even half-a-century to do so. Urban Hindu Bengalis and Cachar Bengalis are on the other hand, particular about their language rights and no reason why they should not be. They, too, are slowly getting culturally assimilated to the typically Assamese psychological make-up and way of life, through various economic, political and social ties, geographical compulsions and inter-penetration of group memories, sentiments and forms of culture.

Under the circumstances, we do not share the conspiracy theory (propounded by Baruah to explain the Asamiyaisation process going on amongst the migrant Muslims), but have faith in the inevitability of the historical integrative process. The linguistic conversion no longer remains a political act. It is an economic act, dictated by the needs of the regional market with its centre at Guwahati. Migrants increasingly find the value of Asamiya as the language of the market place in the Brahmaputra Valley. The Asamiya festival, Bihu, has emerged, like its script, as the secular symbol of Assamese unification. Asamiya folk music, powerfully represented and recreated by Bhupen Hazarika, has cast its spell over Bengali light music.

One can readily agree with Baruah when he says that the principle of linguistic states in India has, amongst other factors, held out the promise of an Asamiya homeland. Not the Asamiyas alone, others too within the state of Assam and outside it have similar aspirations for a homeland. The national formations are still in a melting pot; and these are expected to take their final appropriate shapes only after consistent democracy and autonomisation are accepted as basic principles of state organization.

Under the circumstances, two possibilities of regional national development are open before us in the present state of Assam: (i) The Asamiyas, the Karbis, the Dimasas and the Cachar Bengalis continuing to share the same autonomous state on the basis of their historically evolved understandings, so far achieved in an attempt to resolve national contradictions, or (ii) the Asamiyas limiting the unilingual state concept strictly to only the homogeneous Asamiya-speaking area.

The formation of a state-wise Assamese nationality through an integration of the Asamiyas, the Cachar-

Bengalis, the Karbis, the Dimasas and other tribal national formations on the Swiss model, is not an impossible thing. Wide acceptance of the Assam State Language Act, 1961, declaring Asamiya the official language of the state, and Bengali of Cachar, and the introduction of Asamiya in 1972 as the medium of instruction at the level of University education (with English as an alternative medium) - these resulted from a common concern of the Cachar-Bengalis and the Asamiyas for the preservation for their age-old historical association. If consistent democracy with autonomisation is practised, there is no reason why the Asamiyas, Bengalis, Karbis, Dimasas, Mishings and Bodo-Kacharis could not fulfill their cultural and linguistic aspirations, while sharing the same state. Even now the Karbis and the Dimasas enjoy a considerable degree of territorial autonomy in their respective territories, under the provisions of the Sixth Schedule.

The other possibility open before the people is to allow little nationalism to degenerate into chauvinism and go through further "territorial fragmentation just so that what is left of their state can unambiguously be a state of their own"; in other words, to retreat to the old, more or less stable boundaries of the late 17th century Ahom Kingdom, for achieving an unadulterated Asamiya homeland. The Asam Sahitya Sabha led, with its aggressive linguistic policies in the past, to this fragmentation. By its insistence on the adoption of Asamiya as the only medium of instruction in all schools, during the currency of the present movement, it is again preparing the ground for another fragmentation.

Given the two possibilities, the Marxists surely opt for the first and go on working for a larger territorial base for the regional state so that a bigger Asamiya/Assamese nationality is developed slowly through a process of voluntary integration, with Asamiya continuing to be the official language of the state and the medium of higher education, with English as an alternative medium (as long as the linguistic minorities insist on it) in the universities.

Table 6.4: Average Per Capita Income of Select States

State	*Comparable Estimates of Per Capita Domestic Product at State Current Prices, 1975-76 (Rupees)*	*Average Per Capita Income 1973-74 to 1975-76 (Rupees)*	*Percentage of Literacy (Per Cent)*
Punjab	1688	1586	34
Haryana	1514	1399	27
Maharashtra	1455	1349	39
West Bengal	1100	1033	33
Kerala	1000	948	60
Rajasthan	873	853	19
Orissa	834	793	26
Assam	848	791	29
Madhya Pradesh	790	776	22
Uttar Pradesh	727	715	22
Bihar	669	645	20

Source: Report of the 7th Finance Commission, 1978, cited in *Basic Statistics of North Eastern Region,* NE Secretariat, Shillong, February 1980, pp. 65-66; and *Statistical Handbook,* Assam 1978 Directorate of Economics and Statistics, Govt. of Assam, Gauhati, p. 281.

V

Communists and the Anti-Foreigner Upsurge

T. Mishra highlights Assam in her articles as a colonial hinterland; G. Pardeshi, as an internal colony within the national exploitative system; and H. Gohain, as an underdeveloped area, depressed in the process of the law of uneven development of capitalism and its colonial legacy. There is a consensus among the leftists that the colonial legacy of an exclusively raw material supplying role still persists in Assam, serving the interests of the Indian big bourgeoisie and feudal exploiters. This is indeed one of the basic points of the agitation and propaganda communists of all shades have been carrying on in Assam since Independence.

Most of them however would not agree with Misra when she, like Omvedt, characterizes the parochial and chauvinist outbursts as the "movements for self-determination (economic and political) of the oppressed and backward nationalities of India". For, in Marxist terminology, self-determination involves the right to secede and this is unwarranted by the situation unaccompanied by an economically, culturally and politically dominant nationality within our multinational Indian state.

No demand for self-determination or even more power for the state has been raised from the organized platform of the movement. Its almost sole emphasis is on expulsion of a very big proportion of Assam's population, irrespective of their local birth and/or long residence. How could then the communists join the mass mobilisations in favour of this specific central demand and against the basic human rights of a fourth of the population, going back on the ideals of Marxism-Leninism, as explained above?

The Bengalis, or, for that matter, the Nepalis are not an oppressor nationality in their relationship with the Asamiyas; nor are the Asamiyas, in relation to the plains tribals. There are only specific contradictions, chauvinism and local nationalism among them that need to be overcome. In China for instance, Han chauvinism was pretty bad, but that did not justify Tibetan local nationalism. In China, the communists fought both and defended the working peoples irrespective of their nationality.

The Bengalis are neither dominant in the economy nor in the state machinery. The Indian big business is represented by the Marwaris in Assam, and the state power, also, largely by non-Bengalis. Even in the professions, government services, universities and the cultural field, the Bengalis have lost their pre-Independence position of dominance to the Asamiyas long back; they still retain it only in some of the Central government establishments. How is it, then, that more than 90 per cent of those declared undesirable as citizens happen to be Bengalis? By accidental circumstances? If so, how is it, then, that worn-out myths and past anti-Bengali prejudices are being raked up afresh during the movement by the Gana Sangram Parishad and its constituents? All these questions need an answer, before any honest attempt is made to assess the communists' role vis-a-vis the movement. It goes to the credit of Misra that she has given also one instance as to how Jyotirmoy Basu, a CPI (M) MP, used the floor of the Parliament to give voice to the agonies of Assam.

The plight of Assam, indeed the whole of northeast region, is pretty bad under the big business rule and exploitation. But the same big business is also exploiting Bihar, Orissa, Madhya Pradesh, Uttar Pradesh and West Bengal; in fact, all parts of India in varying degrees. Rajasthan, the home of Marwari capital, too, is one of India's relatively more backward states, both economically and culturally. A comparison of the average per capital incomes and literacy rates of states (Table 4) suggests that some of them, too, have reasons to be discontented. Sometime back, Bihar's case was represented in a book with the sub-title "Colony within a Colony", and the title of Ranajit Roy's book on West Bengal is "*Agonies of West Bengal*". Under the circumstances, the interests of the toiling masses in all these states and all over India are identical - to defeat big business policies by their united struggles.

The present movement, instead of uniting the toiling masses of various castes, creeds and languages in an anti-feudal, anti-monopolist struggle has divided them. It has made tea labour suspicious of the motives of the movement. It denied 20,000 organised plywood workers their basic right to work for a living since August. Three demands in the 16-point charter of demands canvassed by the AASU were anti-tribal. All these apart, the leaders of the movement have taken an active role in breaking up trade unions, for reasons already explained.

Similarly, the land nexus of the movement relates to the interests of the Asamiya landlords rather than of the peasantry, particularly in Lower Assam. The leftists came in a sizeable number in the Assam Legislature in 1978, with 24 seats in a

126-member house and 11 per cent of valid votes. Landlord circles had apprehensions that the left would now press for the implementation of the Land Ceiling Act, long kept in abeyance by the Assam government, and for new legislation in defence of the tenant farmers' rights on the West Bengal model and of tribal peasants' interests in protected tribal blocs on the Tripura model. Besides, the CPI (M)'s influence was rapidly increasing among Asamiya poor peasants in notorious landlord-infested areas. All these, amongst other factors, prompted the landlords - many of them are also salaried and professional people or moneylenders *(dehan)* - to become true sons of mother Assam overnight, forgetting their all-India party ties. This is how the land nexus and anti-tenant character of the movement as well as the overnight disappearance of local bodies of some all-India parties should be explained. It is not the case of landlords merely taking advantage of otherwise a noble movement. On the contrary, the landlords, in league with Asamiya capitalists saw to it that a fierce movement with an anti-Bengali and anti-communist edge was created so that they could get rid of undesirable elements on their farms and keep the toiling peasants divided. One finds such landlords and their sons and daughters at all levels of the Gana Sangram Parishad. Unfortunately the ideology of Misra and Baruah, though differing in language and jargons, is at once a rationalization of the Asamiya upper classes' interests and a view of social reality from their class standpoint.

Because of the largely communal (caste Hindu) and pro-landlord stance of the movement in terms of non-secular symbols and even secular demands (this explains why the RSS has emerged as a friend of the movement), the social base of the movement went on narrowing down. The plantation labour class apart, large sections of Asamiya Muslims and plains tribals, too, who had been initially with the movement, are now opposed to it. Syed Abdul Malik, MP, and ex-secretary, ex-president and life-long associate of the Asam Sahitya Sabha who, himself, had hailed the earlier language movement as "stone given life", for instance, has gone against the present movement.

Tribal peasants want all transferred lands restored to their original tribal proprietors from the clutches of intruders, irrespective of their citizenship status, in the tribal belt constituted of 31 reserved blocks. They also want education of their children through their mother tongues at the school stage. Seeing that the movement is not sympathetic to these demands, they are now increasingly turning hostile to it. L. Panging, a plains tribal youth leader, has for instance observed recently:

> Yes there are foreigners in Assam, they need to be expelled. The tribal people are aware that it is a major problem. But the demand for deportation of foreign infiltrators is a demand of secondary importance, i.e., a short-term demand.... It cannot be a last ditch battle for the survival of Assam, unless the Assamese people are going to be submerged in milk and honey following the expulsion of the foreigners. (Trans from *Sampratik Samayikii,* April-May 1980.)

We repeat our conclusion that the present movement in Assam is essentially national in form (at least it was so at the outset) and, despite mass participation, is reactionary and undemocratic in content. The methods of the movement are proto-fascist, and an involvement of foreign agents as a peripheral force in it is not impossible. Under the circumstances, there was no scope for the leftists to be within it or to fraternize with it. A section of the CPI (M-L) students led by Uttam Barthakur tried to democratize AASU and remain with it in the movement, despite reservations, only to burn their fingers. They found the platform too hot and they quit it. It is not by expelling, but by assimilating the settlers that the bulk of the problem could be resolved. A powerful process of voluntary integration is already there, and the communists apparently should want not to halt, but to expedite it through the maintenance of national peace under any cost. Even in the past, when the Brahmaputra Valley and Cachar were at loggerheads over the language issue in 1960, the united CPI of those days helped dissolve the tension with its compromise formula which was acceptable to all and is still working. Now also they are in favour of a negotiated political settlement, since the sensitivities of a whole people and their injured feelings, for reasons real and imaginary, are involved. Upper class women alone did not come out on the streets, nor is the movement picnic-style as an embittered Jyoti Basu told us once in despair this year. It is dangerous because it has a mass character.

History has shown that even in Germany and Italy during the inter-war period, much stronger communist movements had temporarily collapsed like a house of cards when injured national feelings gave vent to blind forces of chauvinism and obscurantism in the form of anti-Jewish pogroms and anti-left storm-troopers. The cudgel of chauvinism being based on a small nationality within a federal State, its proto-fascist tendency is a passing phase in Assam. But the harm done meanwhile is immense. Forces of authoritarian ism have been consciously or inadvertently strengthened in Assam by the movement by its attacks on democratic rights of the people and its handing over of the initiative for a settlement to Delhi[2]. As space does not permit, we propose to present a more comprehensive review of Assam's left movement in relation to the national question and the upsurge - both its weaknesses and points of strength - in course of an article to follow.

REFERENCES

1. Incidentally, Gail Omvedt is totally mistaken to suggest in her *Frontier* (June 7,1980} article that plough-less shifting cultivation continued to be an important mode of agriculture until the Bengali migrant peasants broke it down. In fact the plough and wet rice culture was the basis of the expanding Ahom and other Kingdoms in medieval northeast India. Hoe and digging stick culture survived only in the hills and persisted feebly in some remote pockets on the Assam plains. Plough-less shifting cultivation was already a thing of the past in these plains when the migrants arrived. Bengali migrant peasants were generally more skilled, but not in every respect. For instance, the tribal peasant in some areas made use of techniques of gravitational irrigation to grow wet rice, but not the Bengalis. However, some

features of tribalism, such as slash-and-burn and land rotation, survived in combination with plough-tilling on lands not suitable for permanent wet rice cultivation. It is these features which the migrant peasants intervened with. The latter contributed towards the spread of double cropping, new crops such as jute, mung, pulse and new varieties of vegetables, etc., and also new techniques such as the Baroj method of betel-vine cultivation and a relatively advanced fishing technology. If the tea labour migration into plantations had made the Brahmaputra Valley rice-short in the 19th century, the Bengali peasant migration of the 20th century made it more than self-sufficient in rice.

2. As some of the articles on Assam published during this year in *EPW,* e.g., those by K.M. Sarma and S.K. Dass reproduce much of the relevant Census statistics in tabular form, our statistical tables are kept to the minimum.

7

The Assam Question: A Historical Perspective A Comment*

—***Lily Bara***

Assam was never a part of the process of nation building in India, and this fact had nothing to do with "settled agriculture" in Assam, as K.M. Sharma tries to argue. *(EPW,* August 2). Except in the hills the slash and burn method of agriculture has not been followed in the Brahmaputra Valley in the last fifteen hundred years. One has simply to go through the accounts of Yuan Chwang, the famous Chinese scholar-traveller and the subsequent references to Assam including those of Talish Shahabuddin, the famous Persian annalist to realize this. By and large settled agriculture has existed in the Brahmaputra Valley throughout the last several centuries.

Could division of labour be complete in a system other than capitalism? Assam's in the main was a peasant economy; so division of labour was ruled out. The Ahoms contributed a lot to the development and use of the Assamese language; the few hundreds of them, who had belonged to the main wave of

* *EPW,* Vol. XV, No. 49, December 6, 1980, pp. 2063-64

immigrants from the Southern part of China ultimately crossed the Patkai Hills in the beginning of the 13th century and with Sukapha at the head settled down in the plains washed by the three tributaries of the Brahmaputra namely the Dihing, the Disang and the Dikhou. They did not meet much resistance from the local people belonging to such communities as Chutiyas, Barahis, Kacharis, etc. By 1238 the Ahom chief, Sukapha, had consolidated his rule over the territory between the Luhit and the Disoi. Only after 170 years did the Tipamiya and Nara chiefs make abortive attempts to resist the Ahoms. Through the adoption of the Assamese language and intermarriage with the local people the Ahoms helped social and political unification and contributed to the growth of the Assamese nationality.

Whether one likes it or not Assam was a nation with an elective monarchy for about six hundred years. When the Britishers annexed Assam in 1826 they destroyed Assam's sovereignty but could not interfere with the basic identity of the indigenous residents.

The Ahom system of government was a class by itself. To call it a form of oriental despotism (as Sharma does) is to betray ignorance of the entire socio-economic and political history of Assam. The dynastic principle was important, but not decisive. There were occasions when this principle was relegated to the background, and the principle of fitness got precedence. As in the case of the king the other officials of the state were in the main from particular clans or dynasties, none of which had its leader as such. The titles that the officials bore were, as a rule, conferred on persons of proven qualities and in turn these officials could exercise their authority through the operation of the collective will inherent in the institution of the *met* (The Panchayat in Assam). The entire system was decentralized with the *mels* of local officials having decisive role with the subsequent endorsement from the state council. Neither the king nor the officials as individuals could exercise decisive power. Naturally, the system of government suffered from various defects such as the lack of a properly organized bureaucracy and a system of laws, the absence of a common medium of computation, the non-use of administrative, deliberative and judicial records and complete absence at any level of the separation of powers. In addition to these defects the fact that the Ahoms did not keep a strong standing army but depended on the militia whose members were not formally remunerated weakened the state.

Despite these weaknesses, the Ahom system of government was not challenged as such, although there were some instances of vassals in outlying areas defying the suzerainty of the monarch at times but capitulating to him subsequently after defeat in battle. Only one rebellion, that of the Moamarias in 1809, shook the entire state to its foundation. The so-called Indian system of feudalism could never infiltrate the major part of Assam and did not pose a challenge to the Ahom system of government. The Moamaria rebellion was engineered by people who could not tolerate the coercive methods adopted at the behest of Queen Phuleswari by a handful of indiscreet officials headed by Kirti Chandra Barbarua to revive popular respect towards the Sakta cult of Hinduism, which had suffered greatly on account of the spread of Vaishnavism in the Brahmaputra Valley.

The Ahom system of government was neither fully tribal nor fully oligarchic. The process of "Assamese nation building" did not take place "in the last century and a half; the Assamese nation had attained maturity as early as the 17th century, and the composite Assamese language and culture had developed through the fusion of various dialects and cultures of local communities long before the Ahoms came.

ASSAM IN BRITISH PERIOD

Nowhere in his article does Sharma refer to the brace exploits of patriots like Piyali Phukan against the British Government; nor has he mentioned the rebellious activities of Maniram Dewan. According to his analysis the initial "rage against foreign imperialist domination" acquired "an added anti-Bengali and anti-non-Assamese" character, and that "anti-imperialist" and anti-Bengali aspects of "Assamese nationalism" were contradictory. But how can there be a contradiction between a criminal and his accomplice? What made the anti-imperialist Bengalis accompany the British imperialists to Assam and abet them in their crimes? Why did they attempt to pulverise Assam both culturally and politically? A few amongst them might be innocent, but by their silent acquiescence to the perfidious manipulations against the indigenous people of Assam, they became accomplices in the imperialist crime of exploitation. The majority of the Assamese intellectuals did not consider the British imperialists "saviours", though some amongst them openly appreciated the British for restoring order after the Burmese invasion.

In regard to the autochthons in hills and other inaccessible areas, the British adopted the policy of keeping them in isolation and using them for various purposes including as political counterweight. Propagation of Christianity and "the importation of lakhs of workers from Bengal, Bihar, Orissa, central India and Madras Presidency" had nothing to do with the question of the "Development of the Assamese Nation". It is true that these two elements of religion and economy belonging to the superstructure and basis did create some problems for the people of Assam, but by themselves they did not produce hostility between those who spoke Assamese and those who did not. Sharma has not cited any figures to substantiate his charge that "many Black tribal communities" have suffered seriously because of "attacks by Assamese chauvinism". The very few clashes between indigenous peasants and the tea garden workers till today have been caused mainly by insignificant factors such as the lack of proper demarcation of land, stealing of cattle or goats, damage to crops, drunkenness on market days or cash-making days, eve-teasing or love-making in which village youngmen and tea garden damsels are involved. The question of Bengali Muslims migrating to settle in the "uncultivated riverine tracts along the Brahmaputra" was entirely different from the question of the tea garden workers most of whom mere brought by agents on contract basis and as such were closely linked with the production of tea. Whereas the Muslim and Hindu immigrants after settling in Assam have become owners of landed property, houses and in some cases even commercial establishments, plantation workers have not possessed anything as such, and their continuance in the jobs in the tea gardens have always been dependent on their size and capacity to absorb them.

CENSUS MYSTERIES

Sharma should have quoted all the relevant data from census reports since 1871 and should not have confined himself only to the percentage increases of linguistic groups since 1911. The demographic data from 1871 to 1931 proved again and again that the polyglot population of the six districts of the Brahmaputra Valley could never exceed the Bengali speaking population of Sylhet and Cachar districts of the Surma valley. According to the 1931 Census, there were 19,81,369 Assamese speaking people as against 10,87,776 Bengali speaking people in the Brahmaputra Valley. This figure revealed around 30 per cent increase of the Assamese population over a forty year period. But by 1961 Assamese speaking people were supposed to have increased more than threefold to reach the staggering number of 67,31,378 whereas during the same very period the Bengali speaking people were supposed to have decreased to 8,99,465 - this was in spite of fact that more than 22,000 "refugees" were officially rehabilitated in the region. Obviously, large numbers of Bengalis and other non-Assamese people had returned Assamese as their mother tongue. It was not the result of assimilation, forced or otherwise, but a conspiracy to flatter the Assamese through deception. The fact is, a large section of the immigrants in Assam have succeeded in securing political dividends under the ruse of accepting Assamese language while at the same time sponsoring a mushroom growth of Bengali medium schools everywhere in Assam.

Sharma has made many other contradictory assertions: On the one hand he refers to "underdeveloped division of labour" and "extremely weak feudal development"; at the same time he also speaks of "bourgeois landlord classes of the Assamese people". If the Assamese "bourgeois landlord" classes have been the strength of their own and have to depend solely on the government machinery to advance their class interest, how can they be called a "bourgeois landlord" class? And in spite of "the Assamese bourgeoisie growing rich" through "the wholesale plunder of the exchequer", they do not find a place among the capitalists in India, whereas in 1951 itself as many as 320 Bengalis were directors of companies and as many as 20 of these companies were solely owned by them (*The Economic Development of India* by Brain Davey, p. 99).

Neither landlords nor the bourgeoisie in Assam can be compared with their counterparts in any other state in India. There is not a single millionaire among the Assamese people. There are less than 10,000 people among them owning 10 hectares of land or above. The rulers of Delhi since the British days have found their faithful agents in Assam to carry out their behests; but this does not necessarily mean that these agents possess the same class characteristics as are possessed by their counterparts in Bengal, Bihar, U.P. Anyway, in the nature of India's political system no local agent has been able to dominate a state government machinery.

8

Little Nationalism Turned Chauvinist
A Comment*

—Udayon Misra

Amalendu Guha, ('Little Nationalism Turned Chauvinist', *EPW,* Special Number, October 1980) seems to have picked up more cudgels against the Assam movement than he can actually wield. In his zeal to drive home the point that the current movement in Assam is nothing but a chauvinist upsurge, Guha has not only resorted to muddled theorizing and self-contradictory statements but also to suppression and distortion of facts.

(1) Guha suggests that the separation of Sylhet from Assam was chiefly the result of the efforts of the Assamese little nationalists and that "after Sylhet was shaken off its back" the "Asamiya middle class emerged stronger and more ambitious than ever", concealing the fact that till, 1874 Sylhet was never a part of Assam. And that Sylhet was, to quote Guha himself, "historically as well as ethnically an integral part of Bengal" *(Planter-Raj to Swaraj,* 1977, p. 27).

---

* EPW, Vol. XVI, No. 8, February 21,1981, pp. 290-92.

It was only in 1874 that Sylhet was incorporated into the province of Assam to make the latter economically viable. There was wide scale protest in Sylhet against its separation from Bengal and its incorporation with a "backward region" (*ibid,* pp. 112, 127). The Assamese people too wanted Sylhet to be restored to its earlier status as a district of Bengal and "public opinion in both the valleys emerged united on the transfer question" (*ibid,* p. 167). In his article, however, Guha seems to give sole credit to the Asamiya middle class chauvinists for the separation of Sylhet from Assam.

Table 8.1: Distribution of Population in Assamese and Bengali Language

Year	*Assamese Speaking*	*Percentage Variation*	*Bengali Speaking*	*Percentage Variation*
1951	4971229	-	1717381	-
1961	6784271	36.47	2061533	20.04
1971	8904996	31.26	2907100	41.02

(2) According to Guha, the Bengali-speaking population in reconstituted post-1947 Assam declined from 30 per cent in 1951 and 20 per cent in 1971. While referring to this sharp decline in the post-1947 period, Guha should have mentioned that the chief reason behind this was the separation of Sylhet, the most populous Bengali-speaking district, from Assam. At the time of partition, Sylhet alone had a population of approximately 2 million as against the rest of Assam's population of approximately 9 million. Moreover, while comparing population figures of pre-1947 and post-1947 Assam, it must be borne in mind that reconstitution of territory attendant on partition resulted in total changes in the population base of the state. Mere decline in the percentage of the Bengali-speaking population in post-1947 Assam does not prove the point that the Bengali-speaking population "has been growing more modestly". Guha says that during the 1951-71 period the state's Bengali population

expanded only 71 per cent while the Assamese population expanded 80 per cent. The accompanying Table (Source: *Census of India* 1971), however, gives a different picture. Thus, the Bengali-speaking population which increased by only 20.04 per cent in the 1951-60 period showed an increase of 41 per cent during the 1961-70 period. The Assamese speaking population during the 1961-70 period increased by only 31 per cent, despite the fact that a large section of immigrant Bengali Muslims may have returned Assamese as their mother-tongue for political and other considerations.

(3) The specter of Asamiya chauvinism seems to haunt Guha so much that he creates chauvinists even out of some leading Assamese Congressmen of pre-dependence Assam who were known for their all-India outlook. Guha has referred to a speech by Tarunram Phukan, to prove his point. Tarunram Phukan, better known as 'Dehabhakta Phukan' in Assam, was one of those select few Assamese Congressmen who had succeeded in giving an all-India perspective to Congress politics in Assam. In fact many Assamese 'jatiyatabadis' of today allege that but for Tarunram Phukan and Gopinath Bordoloi, Assam would have successfully resisted Indianisation. What is most surprising is that Guha has not only quoted out of context Phukan's address as President of the 1927 session of the Assam Sahitya Sabha, but has given a wrong translation of the sentence which he has put under emphasis: "A *rising nationality shows signs of life by extending domination over others". The original Assamese is: Uthi aha jatir jibanar cin haise parar uparat probhava bistar kara" (Asom Sahitya Sabhar Bhasanawali,* Vol. 1, Jorhat, 1955). A correct translation of this sentence would be: "The sign of life of a rising nationality is the *influence* it extends over others". The word, "prabhava" in Assamese does not mean "domination" and it is puzzling that Guha, with his intimate knowledge of the Assamese language, should make such a slip. To be fair to Phukan, Guha could well have quoted some more passages from the same address wherein Phukan exhorted his countrymen to draw inspiration from the cultural and

spiritual heritage of India and to be inspired by India's national heroes, poets and litterateurs. We fail to understand why Guha is so irked by Phukan's assertion of Assamese nationality as part of the greater Indian nation.

(4) Guha says that the "migrants did not come as conquerors and exploiters but as sources of cheap labour supply to not only the big bourgeoisie, but also to the Asamiya landlords and the rising Asamiya capitalists...... Are not these people mostly independent small peasants, agricultural workers and tenants, and not landlords, in relation to their Asamiya neighbours? If so, the Asamiya nationalism connected with such land relations is gentry nationalism not peasant nationalism". While it is true that a small percentage of immigrant peasants from east Bengal were employed by the local rich peasantry as cheap labour, it would be a gross exaggeration amounting to untruth to say that the overwhelming majority of these immigrants were merely sources of cheap labour. That the immigrant peasants, taking advantage of the Raiyatwari land system of Assam and the land settlement policy of the British, occupied large tracts of fertile land in Brahmaputra Valley, thereby causing increasing pressure on land leading to social conflict is a fact admitted by Guha himself in his book under reference: "All that they wanted was land. From their riverine base, they further pressed themselves forward in all directions in search of more of living space in the *areas held by the autochthons.* It was then that an open clash of interests began to take place" *(ibid,* p. 206, emphasis added). That the clash of interests was not confined to the Asamiya rich peasantry and the immigrants but also involved the urban middle class and the peasant masses is amply substantiated by Guha himself. "If the immigration continued unrestrained, would not the Assamese be turned into a linguistic minority in their own homeland - the Brahmaputra Valley? This was the question which plagued the mind of not only its urban middle classes, but also the *peasant masses.* It was in this context that public attention was focused on the Line System which officials had evolved in response to the situation since 1920" *(ibid,* pp. 205-6). Is not Guha going back on his own

findings in stating today that Asamiya nationalism has no peasant base but is "gentry nationalism"?

It is true that landlords do not migrate in search of land, only the exploited and the landless migrate. But could that be justification enough to encourage and allow large-scale infiltration and occupation of land by migrants (which has continued till the present day) from a region which became part of a separate country over thirty years back? Besides, by giving a landlord-tenant twist to the entire question of the occupation of land by the migrants and the resultant conflict with the autochthons, Guha is trying to confuse readers who are not adequately acquainted with the land-system of Assam. While discussing Assam's land-relations Guha should have at least mentioned the fact that except in Goalpara and Sylhet where there were permanently settled estates, the cultivable land of the region was generally covered by the Raiyatwari tenure.

(5) Guha has tried to show that "neither the overall linguistic nor the religious balance, in terms of proportions internal to the Assamese society, has been affected by the migration movements of 1951 to 1971". The 'quick estimates' made by him unfortunately do not consider the fact that the question of illegal infiltration into Assam cannot be discussed without taking into account the tremendous pressure on cultivable land in the 1951-71 period. According to the recently published 1971 National Atlas, Assam was subjected to the greatest population pressure between 1961 and 1971, with the density of population rising from 138 per sq. km to 186 per sq. km during the decade, a rise of almost 35 per cent. No other state, according to the Atlas, recorded a one-third increase in population density during the decade. Although Guha would ascribe the rise in density to the 'abnormal' rise of the Assamese population, the fact remains that in certain districts such as Nowgong and Kamrup, the local people have been progressively eased out of their land by immigrant settlers. For example, in Nowgong District where the density of population has risen from 156 persons per square kilometer in 1951 to 302 persons per square kilometer in 1971, vast areas

once held by indigenous tribals are today in almost total occupation by immigrants (excepting the few reserved tribal blocks). Even Guha concedes that the "Peoples' demand that Assam should not be burdened with further immigration from foreign lands and that all genuine foreigners .... should be detected and removed is legitimate".

To dismiss the force of nationalism behind the current anti-foreigner movement as 'gentry nationalism' would be to overlook reality. Guha is not able to explain the involvement of large sections of the Assamese peasantry, including plains tribals, in the current movement. Probably Guha is aware that over the years there has been large-scale pauperization amongst the Assamese peasantry in districts like Kamrup and that there has been large-scale transfer of land to rich peasants, a sizeable percentage of whom happen to be immigrants from erstwhile East Pakistan and Bangladesh. It is a fact that in many of the 'char' areas in Kamrup District, Assamese peasants have been compelled by circumstances to sell their land at nominal prices to their immigrant neighbours and to migrate to the Bhutan border.

(6) Guha has suggested assimilation or, rather, the 'Asamiyaisation' of the immigrants as a possible solution to the problem of little nationalism turned chauvinist. According to him, while the Bengali Muslim settlers in the Brahmaputra Valley have displayed unmistakable signs of Asamiyaisation, Urban Bengalis and Cachar Bengalis too "are getting culturally assimilated to the typically Assamese psychological make-up and the way of life, through various economic, political and social ties, geographical compulsions and inter-penetration of group memories, sentiments and forms of culture". While all this may sound very impressive, this talk of 'Asamiyisation' totally overlooks the fact that the Bengalis cannot be grouped into 'Cachar Bengalis', 'Urban Bengalis', etc. Bengalis form part of the Bengali nationality which is marked by a highly developed language and culture of its own. How can Guha, as a Marxist, suggest that the Bengali nationality assimilate itself with the Asamiyas? The question of assimilation of a developed

nationality like the Bengalis with the Assamese cannot be discussed in such simple terms. While discussing the question of assimilation it must be kept in mind that the Bengalis (Hindus as well as Muslims) in Assam are part of a distinct, developed nationality; that they have concentrated themselves in certain 'pockets' in the Brahmaputra Valley, thereby reducing the need to culturally or linguistically assimilate with the neighbouring Assamese; that the process of assimilation which had started in certain immigrant areas has been disrupted by fresh waves of migrants from East Pakistan and Bangladesh; and that in areas where the migrants are not only strong in numbers but are also in possession of vast tracts of land, their urge to assimilate with the indigenous people has been naturally reduced. Assimilation was possible in the case of those Bengalis who came to Assam in the Ahom period and during the early decades of British rule. Lack of numerical strength as well as difficult communication links were some of the important factors which helped this assimilation. But this is not the case with the Bengalis in Assam today who form part of a distinct nationality. Therefore, to suggest that they become Asamiyised is to tread on slippery grounds. Guha himself has in his book under reference dealt in detail about the efforts of the Bengalis in the Brahmaputra Valley to assert their linguistic identity and to turn Assam into a bilingual state. This was only too natural.

Poor and landless peasants who came and settled in the Brahmaputra Valley in the early decades of this century found it convenient to assimilate with the Assamese; but the situation changed as the rate of immigration rapidly increased and the migrants concentrated themselves in certain areas instead spreading out evenly throughout the state. Along with ownership of land came the question of wielding political power and the emerging middle classes as well as the rich peasants among these immigrants came to play an increasingly dominant role. As Guha himself states in one of his unpublished papers, "Amongst the immigrant groups some were both numerically and culturally viable.

Not only that they did respond poorly to the process of assimilation, but they also did aspire for the same dominant role as that of the Assamese in the valley" *(Immigrants and Autochthons in a Plural Society: The Interrelations in the Brahmaputra Valley).* Therefore, to talk of Asamiyisation without taking into account the growing social tension between the Bengali immigrants and the Assamese peasants would be to idealise the entire situation.

(7) Guha has accused the Assam Sahitya Sabha of fanning chauvinist frenzy. He has also praised the Sabha for its good job in getting folk tales in the Mynmensinghia dialect of East Bengal translated into Assamese. Perhaps this explains the contradictory pulls exerted by the Sabha at different periods of its existence on intellectuals of varying shades. Guha himself presided over the History Session of the Sabha held at Titabar a few years ago. May be he was not particularly aware of the Sabha's chauvinistic role at that time.

(8) It is amazing that Guha sees parallels between situations as radically different as eighteenth century Assam under the Ahoms, the rise of fascism in Germany and the current anti-foreigner movement in Assam.

Lastly, his rather long article is totally silent on state violence let loose on the people of Assam during the past year and a half. Guha has nothing to say against the adoption of measures like the Disturbed Areas Act, the Armed Forces (Special Powers) Act, the Maintenance of Essential Services Act, and the lathi-charges and firings on largely peaceful demonstrators - Guha's silence on such .curbs on the rights of the people appears to be in line with the open approval of such repressive measures in Assam as necessary "administrative measures" by CPI (M) leaders like Jyoti Basu, Samar Mukherjee and Nripen Chakravarty. Surely, the use of the law-enforcing machinery to curb the spread of communal violence and its use to suppress peaceful protest cannot be viewed in the same light. Guha's assessment of the Assam movement need not have stood in the way of expressing his disapproval of State repression.

9

Little Nationalism Turned Chauvinist
A Comment*

—Hiren Gohain

There can be little dispute about much of Amalendu Guha's sober and patient analysis of the Assam Movement (Special Number, October 1980). But I have certain reservations and criticisms about the general direction of the argument. Such criticism does not follow from opportunism, but from a close observation in the field where time is ripe for a leftist initiative. Though Guha's article is an exception, one gets uneasy about the spate of statistics covering up a reluctance to face the issue squarely in many of the recent articles on Assam. Let me try therefore to give a plain account of the issues as they strike me.

It is interesting to recall that the movement on the issue of the medium of university instruction that had rocked Assam in 1972 anticipated many of the morbid symptoms of the present movement on a smaller scale. Yet, at that time Amalendu Guha had found in it certain "genuine democratic

* *EPW,* Vol. XVI, No. 9, February 28, 1981, pp. 339-40.

and national tendencies", distorted by a malevolent press. But in his opinion the present movement is entirely fascist and the only thing to do about it is to crush it. I have also said on a number of previous occasions that the movement has a fascist form. But now that the danger to the left organizations and ideas from the movement has somewhat receded, it is necessary to re-examine both the movement in general and the role of the left.

Social movements do not take place in a vacuum, and their definite concrete consequences may not be shrugged off merely with an abstract commitment to leftist ideology. While Sanjib Baruah's rationalization of the Assamese middle-class aspirations and anxieties ('unilingual state', etc) is a chimerical guide to action, leftist thinking on the Assam movement has not been particularly fruitful. While there have been loud complaints about the Centre's callous temporization on the present movement, it has not been seen as a mark of crisis in Centre's relation to the north-east. In fact during the previous decades, the Centre had silently delegated to the largely caste-Hindu Assamese elite the role of the gendarme in the north-east. The Assamese ruling elite had always played that role with gusto, to the point of wielding the *danda* on the aspirations of all the weaker nationalities of the region. The present movement very definitely carries the hangover from such hegemonist sprees of the past. Since the middle-class has woken up to a situation now when the scope for such hegemony has shrunk, it has in sheer desperation adopted fascist tactics. In so far as such tactics include attacks on the left, both the BJP and the Congress (I), parties of the Indian big bourgeoisie, connive at if not encourage them. But aspirants for radical sainthood had better digested the unpalatable fact that the Congress (I), at least on paper, has opposed the oppression of the minorities. The BJP on the other hand does not breathe a word about it. But both the parties are keen to acquire some stakes in the movement, which indicates that the movement is not really directed against the big bourgeoisie.

Granted all this, they still fail to explain the extent and quality of mass-participation in the movement. Once the present movement dies down, the left may perhaps be able to resume its interrupted progress in Assam, on the basis of issues relating to the economics and politics of the whole country. But that may not prelude the possibility of yet another big upsurge in the near future on problems the Assamese people think peculiarly their own.

Let me suggest an analogy. The leadership of the Afghan people's movement against foreign occupation of their country may be in the hands of the Islamic fundamentalists. And these may indeed be guided by the CIA, which certainly bodes ill for that unfortunate country. But that by itself certainly does not turn the problem into a non-issue. There are grounds for believing that in the absence of leftist initiative on the sensitive questions such unhappy regions have become the hot-bed of reactionary mass-movements. Of course it does not follow at all that the left should make up for its earlier apathy by joining the bandwagon belatedly. That could only be the worst kind of tailism. Besides, the left must consider and affirm aspects of the situation totally ignored by the fanatics of those movements. In the case of Assam, one can easily think of such aspects as the unity of the peoples of India, security for the minorities, intervention of foreign powers, fascist distortion of the methods and aims of the movement. But it ought not to ignore the grievances and demands in question, but make a vigorous, in-depth study of their roots and devise methods of struggle for winning the support of the aggrieved masses.

Here it must be said that the leftists' flair for reducing everything to a narrow economic basis is inadequate and disastrous. The notion that since the peoples in the north-east have been economically neglected, they have been seduced by trouble-mongers into secessionism is singularly simple-minded. The awakening masses of India at this stage of their development are bound to perceive their problems in a national form. As surely as the Vietnamese and the Chinese, the weaker nationalities of India tend to consider their underdevelopment and stagnation not only as a colonial legacy but also as a continuation of national oppression in another form. They feel they have fallen out of step with the advanced part of the world. Some of them have an additional worry that forces beyond their control may imperil their very existence as separate national groups.

Consider the Assamese outcry against immigration. It is evident that they are not simply worried by the presence of 'foreigners' - though the present movement has adopted the slogan on tactical grounds. In fact, the influx of Hindi-speaking people in large numbers may have the same perilous consequences. The main worry of the Assamese is that they are not in a position economically or politically to regulate such immigration. During the colonial times they could not regulate immigration because the imperialist government could not care less as to what happened to the Assamese. But the Assamese have been made nervous by the fact that the successor-governments in New Delhi have the same outlook as their colonial predecessors. The state government is not left with a significant share of the income from the state, so that it cannot start any major work of development, and the Centre is loftily indifferent to the regional aspirations of the people. Not only are the immigrants the most adventurous and enterprising elements in the areas they come from; their more advanced environment have bred in them greater alertness, resourcefulness and habits of industry and zeal. In fair competition they beat the local candidate hollow. Can the left afford to ignore the injustice of the situation? Why can't it come out with proposals for job-reservation and programmes of extensive local recruitment and training in selected sectors of employment? Why can't it advocate programmes of agricultural and industrial development that would benefit the Assamese mid die-class as much as the working people? The notion of people's democracy does not after all run counter to such tactics, which would in addition have won over part of the local middle-class now solidly aligning itself with the fascist forces. Determined advocacy of such programme will not only expose the Centre and the forces it represents but also disarm local suspicions about communist intentions.

Without going so far as to endorse the thesis of 'colony within a colony', one can point out certain hangovers from the colonial past. As a matter of fact, Assam is not being neglected or forgotten by an allegedly wool-gathering center, but is being systematically drained of her resources to finance development of other regions. The Assamese find themselves in the situation of a client in the matters of economic and political importance, which certainly prevents all-round national growth. Amalendu Guha's contention that there are other similarly placed regions in India does not answer the basic allegation. The oft-repeated leftist plea that there is no national oppression in India, but only varying levels of development, is also patently wrong. Even within Assam, the so-called tribal constituencies have been drawn up by the chauvinistic local elite in such a manner as to rob the tribals of their advantages.

The campaign against the chauvinist and fascist forces in Assam has actually two aspects: (i) exposing, denouncing and resisting manifestations of fascism through upholding ideas of national unity, civil rights and democracy; (ii) affirming and upholding real equality of all nations in the Indian context, to the point of mobilizing support for programmes of development of various national groups, and advocating constitutional safeguards for their identity and welfare. Hegemonistic notions like the 'unilingual state for Assam[1] and separatist ideas gaining popularity among the tribals ought to be combated. But genuine national demands deserve a stout defence.

10

Little Nationalism Turned Chauvinist
A Comment*

—Gail Omvedt

Amalendu Guha's defence of the 'left front' position on Assam *(EPW,* Special Number, October 1980) is welcome because it is the most detailed effort yet by a Marxist academic expert. If such a presentation cannot stand up to empirical evidence or logic, then I would think it is a good indication that the basic political position is itself indefensible.

I am not, like Guha, an expert on Assam. Still, he has taken me as an object of attack and at least admitted that I raised important questions. Since Udayon Misra has already replied on a number of issues (February 21), I would like to restate some points once again - mainly on the national question and on the logical implications of Guha's own position.

Guha attacks me for saying that the Assam movement raises the issues of national self-determination because the Assamese have not made a demand to exercise their right of self-determination to the point of secession. Of course, they

---

* *EPW,* Vol. XVI, No. 13, March 28,1981, pp. 589-90.

have not demanded secession; not every oppressed nationality does - or should. This does not mean that a national question is not involved. Basically, however, Guha's polemic on this point seems just a red herring to cover up the fact that he does not think that the right of self-determination applies at all in the Indian context, even for those who have been fighting for it. This I think is a fundamental point, and without trading quotations from Lenin (Guha's article is an example of doing this in a misleading and out of context way, of which more below), I believe that from a Marxist-Leninist position the right to self-determination is fundamental and the movements of oppressed nationalities to exercise this right against an exploitative State are a crucial part of any general revolutionary movement. So far neither Guha nor others have shown that the difficulty of finding an 'oppressor nation' in India or the readiness of outside interests to interfere in national for other contradictions (which is a factor everywhere in the world today) abrogate such a fundamental right.

Guha's own theory should be closely examined. First, he argues that while before independence there was an objective basis for Asamiya fears of being overwhelmed by outsiders (when the Congress supported the 'democratic and legitimate' demands for state reorganization and the line system to check uncontrolled immigration), now there is none. According to him, now the Bengalis - first the Muslim Bengalis and now the Cachar and urban Bengalis - are being assimilated into the Asamiya nationality and were it not for chauvinism, the tribal minorities would also have been assimilated. According to Guha, "it was only after the 1950s that Assam began to shrink in area with every retreat the Congress made before the tide of rising chauvinism". This would seem to indicate that he feels that even the formation of separate Naga and Mizo states was a chauvinistic mistake. His position seems to be that a large multilingual state (even in a backward semi-feudal region and under an exploitative bourgeois-landlord rule enveloped in imperialist domination) can be a basis for assimilation of the minority linguistic groups into the core linguistic nationality.

This seems a bit fantastic. As Misra points out, the question of assimilation is different in a period of imperialism and capitalist domination than in a feudal (e.g. the Ahom) period. Then, immigrant Bengali speakers and sanskritising tribals could become part of an Asamiya nationality in the process of its formation. Now, Bengali speakers in Assam are linked to a greater Bengali nationality (much larger and more developed in terms of productive forces than the Asamiya nationality), and it is reasonable to think that assimilation processes are much weaker and that even Bengali Muslim settlers who give Assamese as their mother tongue may be doing so for political reasons.

Misra has contested Guha's figures. What even Guha calls the 'abnormal' rise in Asamiya population is due to a large extent to the switch in claimed language of these Bengali Muslims. And if it is true that they are giving Assamese as their language only for political reasons and using it in fact only as a bazaar language, and thus may revert to Bengali (if they have done so under pressure from Assamese chauvinism as opponents of the movement have argued - and this may well be true - the danger is even greater) when given the opportunity, then they are in fact 'true' Bengali speakers and the true Assamese rise is much smaller and that of the Bengalis much greater. There may well be both aspects, genuine assimilation and tactics, to the Bengali Muslim switch, but it seems in any case that however tangled the national question is and however chauvinistic the Assamese response may be, the objective basis for their fears is a real one. (Incidentally also in terms of figures, Guha's comparison of migrants in West Bengal with those in Assam [p. 1709] completely ignores the nationality question).

Guha's own alternative explanation, that the Asamiya nationality has taken on a splendid strength following independence, I simply do not find believable given all the objective indicators of Assam's continuing backwardness, impoverishment and dominance of semi-feudal relations in comparison with other Indian states. How can a middle class suddenly become strong with no material base? And by lumping small capitalists with petty bourgeoisie and calling all a 'middle class' (a bourgeois-academic term, not a Marxist one) he has avoided the issue of dealing with the real class character of the movement's leadership. Finally, by using a quotation from Lenin about Ukraine he confuses the issue even further - for Ukraine, though smaller, was a capitalistically developed region in contrast to Russia, which is why Russian migrants there could become part of a proletariat, taking part in collective production that itself has a base for united action. In contrast, in Assam immigrants seem largely to be competing as peasants for land or as aspirants for petty bourgeois employment of other petty-bourgeois occupations, which hardly lays the basis for any kind of assimilation.

Finally, with no objective basis for any Asamiya grievances, Cuba's 'explanation' of the strength of the current movement is reduced to saying that it is entirely the conspiracy of an aggressive 'middle class' using the media to stir up the population - an explanation which ascribes what again I would have to call fantastic and un-Marxist powers to the media. The bourgeoisie of course always tries to play on divisions among the masses (e.g. the Shiv Sena) but there must be some material basis for this to have any success; the Shiv Sena has not been able to spread into the Maharashtrian countryside because of a lack of this base in contrast to the overwhelming support the Assam movement is admitted to be getting even by its opponents.

It makes much more sense to say that there is a real material base for Asamiya fears of being overrun (including loss of land in districts such as Kamrup and Nowgong, fears of loss of political power, and general backwardness, unemployment, etc.), and that in the absence of left leadership these fears are being voiced by a petty bourgeoisie leadership with definite chauvinist tendencies; and that behind and to some extent regardless of this leadership the force of the Assamese popular movement continues to be a major threat to the Indian State. Nationality issues are complex (and for the left, balancing the needs of different national groups in a single region and giving them an overall revolutionary thrust is never easy) and the leadership of an oppressed national movement can change (as the Naga example is showing); but it can never go to the left if the left refuses to see any legitimate base for that nationality's grievances. In this context, Hiren Gohain's response to Guha (February 28) is surely welcome particularly coming from someone who has maintained his objections to the movement under brutally difficult circumstances, but I have real doubts about whether the current CPI-CPI(M) political line on the national question will allow a creative response.

This brings us finally to the question of the role of the left. Guha, has promised another article on this, so perhaps no foregone conclusions can be made. But so far the only reference for the post-independence period he has cited is that in November 1980, the Assam state committee of the CPI (M) called for a sealing off of the border, etc. Surely the point is not what the Assam unit of the party was doing in 1980 under pressure from the movement, but what the national unit of the CPI (M) or even what the West Bengal unit was saying at that time (and as I remember the Left Front government was taking out ads in dailies across the nation proclaiming the right of any Indian citizen to settle anywhere - except presumably in Marichjhampi), or what the CPI and CPI (M) were saying about the issue years earlier. Since Gohain himself admits that "leftist thinking on the Assam movement has not been entirely fruitful", it is time for those closest to the issue to make a full assessment of the past as well.

11

Little Nationalism Turned Chauvinist
A Comment*

—Sanjib Baruah

Amalendu Guha's 'Little Nationalism Turned Chauvinist' (*EPW*, Special Number, October 1980) is a welcome contribution towards an understanding of an issue which continues to elude a solution and on which left opinion in the country remains far from unanimous. Guha is a pioneer social and economic historian of medieval and modern Assam. No student of Assam can avoid a debt to his writings. His article on the Assam movement raises some important questions on how Marxists and progressives should approach the nationality question in India in general and the Assam issue in particular.

Guha's article begins with the statement that the Assam movement is "undoubtedly related to the national question". Coming from someone who is close to a political tendency which has so far seen the foreigners issue as a pseudo issue. The notion of a crisis of the Assamese nationality's cultural

---

* *EPW*, Vol. XVI, No. 15, April 11, 1981, pp. 676-81.

identity as a myth, and any reference to Assam's tangled nationality question as a rationalization of the AASU position, Guha's 'concession is indeed remarkable'. It is however, as we shall see, more formal than substantive. Recently Hiren Gohain, whose views too had in the past coincided with that of the CPI (M), has also spoken of the left's failures and mistakes in Assam. One such failure he says, is that "the left has underestimated the emotional force of nationalism in a backward environment with an emergent capitalist class" *(EPW,* December 13, 1980). A trend towards self-criticism no matter how half-hearted, can only be welcomed. But it is essential for Marxists to re-evaluate their theories, along with the admission of mistakes and failures. This rejoinder is written in the spirit of a common search for a correct theoretical and political orientation to the subject. It is primarily a theoretical critique of Guha's position, though it simultaneously answers some of the points raised by Guha against my previous articles.

Guha calls the movement "national in form, chauvinist and undemocratic in content and proto-fascist in its methods". Though "undoubtedly related" to the nationality question, the movement does not flow from the question. It has only the "appearance of an Asamiya national movement". Where then lies its content? To explain its content, Guha shifts attention away from the political and cultural levels of Assam's nationality question. There are three points in his major argument. First, the Assam movement is not a struggle for self-determination in Lenin's sense of the term. Second, the notion of a threat to the cultural identity of the Assamese is a myth. Third - and this follows from his first two points - the primary explanation for the Assam movement lies elsewhere; it is a conjunctural crisis of the dominant economic classes in Assam, which explains the "undemocratic content" of the movement.

SELF-DETERMINATION

Guha argues that the Assam movement is not a movement of self-determination. First, because a demand for self-determination in the sense of a demand for outright secession and the formation of a separate state, has not been on the agenda of the Assam movement. Marxists could support such a demand only when it is articulated by the movement itself and when it is aimed against an "oppressor nation". Guha attacks Gail Omvedt and Tilottama Misra for attempting to pass off the "parochial and chauvinist outbursts" as a movement of self-determination. In my articles, I have not used the term self-determination. The use of the term would have inaccurately implied that the Assam movement challenges the integrity of the Indian Union. Instead I have used the concept of sub-nationalism, which is not substantially different from Guha's notion of Little Nationalism. Under the circumstances, Guha's tirade against me for "avoiding the term self-determination" because, as he alleges, my "frame of reference is not multinational India in the Marxist style", is puzzling.

The second reason why Guha thinks the Assam movement is not a legitimate nationality upsurge is that unlike the movements which Lenin had endorsed, the Assam movement is not the nationalism of an oppressed nationality against an oppressor nationality. Indeed, according to his formula, it is impossible to have a legitimate nationality upsurge in contemporary India. For even when it satisfies the first criterion i.e., a demand for secession is explicitly made, it cannot satisfy his second criterion - of being directed against an oppressor nation. For Amalendu Guha rules that after the British had quit, on August 14, 1947, "no particular nationality could be identified as an oppressor nation in relation to other nationalities within the Union as the Russians could be in the Czarist State". Armed with such a general law, it is not surprising that Guha would find that Assam movement is not a legitimate nationality upsurge. In the specific case of Assamese-Bengali relation in Assam, I happen to agree with Guha that the Bengalis, are not an oppressor nation. But Lenin did not set out to give a simple formula for future Marxists when he spoke of oppressor and oppressed nations. "An abstract presentation of the question of nationalism in general is of no use at all. A distinction must be made between the nationalism of an oppressor nation, and that of an oppressed nation, the nationalism of a big nation and that of a small nation"[2]. Even if the Bengalis are not an oppressor nation, there can be little doubt that the Assamese unlike the Bengalis, constitute one of the smaller nationalities in India. As a frontier people, the Assamese nationality is particularly vulnerable to threats to its rights as the 'basic population' of a territory, from exceptional immigration[3]. The Assamese fears and aspirations finding expressions in the present movement are not far-fetched or unreasonable if one takes into account recent Assamese history and the predicament of small frontier peoples everywhere. The example of Tripura, where the basic population has become a minority within three decades and the expanding bigger nationality has come to dominate the entire institutional life of the state, makes the Assamese fears very real. A Tripura like process is unmistakably at work in Assamese political life as well.

It is intriguing why people like Guha constantly harp on the fact - which is itself not beyond dispute - that within Assam the Assamese might still be a majority and the Bengalis a minority (The picture of course changes depending on whether the Immigrant Bengali Muslims are counted as Assamese or as Bengalis). The smallness of the Assamese nationality *vis-a-vis* the Bengalis - a point which has a closer bearing on the Assam crisis - has been over looked. Moreover, the Bengalis may not be an oppressor nation like the Russians in Czarist times, but historically the relations between the Bengalis and the Assamese have elements of domination and subordination. Even if the position of the Bengali language being the official language of Assam and the predominance of Bengalis in the higher echeleons of the bureaucracy are now part of history, structures of domination-subordination do not follow the neat logic of cut-off dates.

The underdevelopment of Assam, which was integrated into India's capitalist economy as a primary commodity producing periphery, adds a third important dimension to the concrete presentation of the Assamese Nationality question. The Assamese movement is the protest movement of a small, non-peripheral region defending its rights as the basic population of a territory, which is historically associated with them. When some people sneer at this upsurge as a "picnic-style movement", it sounds remarkably like what Lenin called Great-nation chauvinism "treating the national movements of small nations with disdain"[4]. In this framework, what bigger nationalities have are heralded as nationalism and renaissance, while similar phenomena occurring in the history of smaller nationalities are called chauvinism and revivals.

THREAT TO IDENTITY: MYTH OR REALITY?

Guha argues that immigration poses no threat to Assamese cultural identity. He finds fault with my assessment that immigration into Assam within a relatively short period of time has few parallels. He has a few clever techniques to demonstrate this. He just cites the figures for migrants from outside the state in West Bengal and Assam in 1961 and 1971. The figures, based on the birth-place data of the census, are higher in West Bengal than in Assam. First, when I said migration to Assam has few parallels, I was referring to the overall impact of migration on the demographic composition of Assam in the course of the present century. The point I had made was little more than what has been said by Guha's statistical ally, Susanta Krishna Dass, who cannot exactly be accused of being an 'Assamese patriot'. According to Dass, "If the proportion of immigrants to indigenous people is taken as the criterion of assessing the weightage of immigration it will be found that next only to Brazil, Assam as a geographical region bears the heaviest impact of outsiders. Also among Indian States, it has accommodated the largest proportionate number of people from elsewhere"[5].

Of course such inferences made from census reports do not provide any clues to the number of foreigners that have come to Assam after independence. But whatever may be the importance of estimating the number of foreigners for AASU and their opponents, for our purposes it is not the most crucial issue to be settled. Second, Guha makes his point by using the birth-place data of the Census. For Assam, for a period when the bulk of the migrants were zealously trying to prove their local roots, the Census is unlikely to be the most reliable of sources.

The analogy with West Bengal is made to show that left politics has accounted for the absence of migration induced tensions in West Bengal. The analogy is not appropriate because unlike the Assamese in Assam, Bengalis face no threat of being outnumbered by migrants in their state as a whole, though the number of migrants in Calcutta is sizeable. Second, unlike Assam where migrants acquire positions of power, the predominance of the Bengali *bhadralok* has kept away migrants from positions of power in West Bengal, Even left parties in West Bengal have pandered to the demands of Bengali nationalism. This probably explains to some extent the CPI (M)'s relative weakness among non-Bengali migrants in West Bengal. A comparative analysis of the composition of successive ministries in West Bengal and Assam would reveal the difference between the roles of migrant politicians in West Bengal and Assam.

Guha's ill-founded conviction that migration of Bengalis poses no threat to the Assamese cultural identity leads him to misread the persistence of a concern for cultural identity as a major theme in the history of Assamese sub-nationalism. Thus, in order to demonstrate that "Asamiya little nationalism had acquired an aggressive tone" as early as the 1920s, Guha quotes from a speech made by Tarunram Phukan in 1927 to underline the 'aggressiveness' of Assamese nationalism. But equally significant is the passage in Phukan's speech that immediately follows the sentence cited by Guha. "Alas!", continued Phukan, "it is otherwise; we are incapable of self-defence today!" The latter sentence should have led Guha to enquire into the context in which Assamese sub-nationalism was growing. The question is whether or not, the Assamese had to defend themselves as early as in 1927. Guha entirely misses the significance of the fact that Phukan's speech was made at a time when migration from East Bengal was reaching record levels and Assamese political protest against it had started.

Guha does not hide his dislike for the cultural identity theme in the history of Assamese sub nationalism. This current in the pre-independence period, according to him, attracted only "government servants, client intellectuals and Congress drop-outs". Some of them were even "encouraged by imperialism". Guha laments the fact that the words and ideas of some of the progressive intellectuals - who cannot be easily dubbed as imperialist stooges - are "being misconstrued, divested of some of their humanist-liberal content and misused for purposes of the movement". The truth is that the threat to Assamese cultural identity from high levels of migration has made the conflict between humanism and nationalism on the one hand, and an apparently parochial concern with Assam's cultural identity, a recurring theme in Assamese intellectual life. People like Ambikagiri Roychaudhuri cannot just be dismissed as 'congress drop-outs'. A fiery nationalist and progressive who wrote the inaugural song for the Pandu session of the Indian National Congress, Ambikagiri died *a* lonely, embittered man in 1967. He was perhaps slightly ahead of his times in expecting the Assamese to rise up in protest against the illegal influx from East Pakistan long before the upsurge of 1979-80. Moreover, the term nationalist drop-outs should not carry a pejorative connotation to Marxists. The dilemma between a concern for broader ideals and for the Assamese predicament occurs even in the songs of Bhupen Hazarika, whose appeal across the Bengali-Assamese divide has been noted by Guha.

Guha gets rather carried away by Census Reports. Contrary to Assamese fears, he discovers that the Asamiya society and culture, "like Pisa's leaning tower . . . Still maintains its tall existence and even grows a rate faster than in the case of any other linguistic group in India." Guha perhaps has for too long only gazed in admiration at the peculiar ethnic structure that has evolved in Assam as a result of mostly unassimilated immigration, rather than inquire into the sources of its cohesion. How long Pisa's tower would have survived if it was built with paper and card board - the stuff that Census Reports are made of - is anybody's guess.

THE CLASS AXIS

After theoretically ruling out the possibility of there being any legitimate national upsurges in contemporary India and dismissing the Assamese fears of a threat to identity as a nightmare that a compulsory reading of Census Reports might end, it only remains for Guha to locate the Assam movement as an epiphenomenon, reducible to the economic base. This is only consistent with his 'Marxist style'. Amalendu Guha accuses me of focusing not on social classes, but on not-too-fundamental categories such as ethnicity, demographic imbalance and plural society. The logic of political power that I have emphasized says Guha, "cannot be autonomous in operation, it requires the mediation of a class or class-in-making in the need for that" political power". Thus far one can only be impressed by Guha's fidelity to the Marxist method. But what are the social classes, which according to Guha, have mediated in the Assam movement? Both at the national and the regional levels Guha tells us, the "emergence of nationalism was a middle-class phenomena". The "middle positions" of the social pyramid, he says in an attempt to define the middle class, "were held by Indian industrialists, traders, petty landlords and various sections of the petty bourgeoisie, urban and rural". This motley crowd is portrayed as a hegemonic class. "A middle class", says Guha, "wants to project its own interests as the interests of a large group so that the latter could be politically mobilized in the struggle for power". But the theoretical question is, can such a "class" be a hegemonic class, even if it wants to be? To argue from class intentions to political outcomes is the bane of vulgar Marxism. Guha wants us to believe that in this middle class search for hegemony "Indian nationalism as well as regional nationalism, originated". The hegemonic class of the Indian national movement, according to Guha, was not the nascent Indian bourgeoisie but the Indian middle class. This is certainly more than what any Marxist had so far granted to this motley crowd. The source of Guha's confusion is not far to seek. For in the name of a Marxist class analysis he sneaks into his paper a category which is rooted not in the Marxist theories of mode of production, but in the sociological theories of social stratification. It is not surprising that Guha is forced to take a liberal, non-Marxist view of the Indian nationalist movement. A theoretically illegitimate marriage between Marx and Weber cannot escape its logical conclusions.

Within the Marxist tradition, it is problematical to attribute to the "middle class" the capacity to have its "own" ideological/political project, not to speak of that project becoming hegemonic. The ideology of the petty bourgeoisie can only consist of incorporation of its own ideological elements into the ideological projects of the two basic classes in a capitalist social formation - capitalists and workers[6]. Second, Guha has followed an intellectual tradition which has thought of Fascism as the ideology of the petty-bourgeoisie. Guha has mercifully fallen short of calling the Assam movement 'Fascist'; it has only an "undemocratic content" and "proto-fascist" methods. Nonetheless, the assumption that the particular classes have particular ideologies (the working class supports socialism and petty-bourgeoisie supports fascism) is problematical. Aren't there historical conjunctures where the working classes have supported Fascism or the petty-bourgeoisie has supported socialism? Only a rigorous analysis of concrete situations, which themselves have an effect on ideological and political practices, can tell us if the-petty-bourgeoisie in a particular situation supports "proto-fascism". Third, what is the source of cohesion of the 'middle class'? There are groups within it who occupy conflicting positions in the production process. There is no *a priori* reason why 'professional and service-holders', for instance, should support the regional nationalism of the small capitalists as Guha suggests and not the nationalism of the big bourgeoisie.

Let us briefly examine how Guha locates the class axis of the Assam movement. In order to define the middle class in the particular context of Assam, Guha goes back to the pyramid of social stratification. He begins at the top and strikes out the big bourgeoisie, for in Assam it is North Indian and is in collaboration with foreign capital. There is no Asamiya big bourgeoisie. Even the next stratum is eliminated in the Assamese case, because of the middle bourgeoisie in Assam, barely six of them speak Assamese! The Assamese middle class, therefore Guha concludes, is "virtually constituted of small capitalists, and other sections of the petty-bourgeoisie including professionals and service-holders, many of whom are also simultaneously small landlords". Unfortunately, Guha does not even pause to ask if Assam's relative backwardness, which shows up in the weakness of some of the classes, could have produced a situation different from that in other states. The leadership of the Assam movement, says Guha, "represent the Asamiya middle class or classes". Why did this class suddenly feel the need for a movement against foreigners? Around 1978, Guha seems to tell us, the Asamiya middle class faced a conjunctural crisis, "Hardpressed by big capital from above and the rising labour and peasant movement from below .... The Asamiya upper classes are terribly agitated about the economic stagnation. . . . Incapable of competing with big capital, they aspire to monopolise the small industries, petty trade and the profession and services". Their survival could be ensured by the programme of the present movement which could eliminate Bengali and other competitors, ensure unhindered labour exploitation and control over state administration - the real aims of the Assam movement. It is this which explains the "anti-democratic" and anti-working class content of the movement. I have stressed in my earlier articles that the attacks on leftists - which need to be condemned in no uncertain terms - reflect not the primary logic of the movement, but an aspect which a different orientation on the part of the left towards the movement might have avoided.

One notices that Guha considerably expands on his notion of the middle class when it comes to explaining the Assam movement. At places he -uses terms such as 'upper classes' or 'bourgeois-landlord chauvinists' - terms which include, apart from the middle classes, some gate-crashers from the top stratum. Guha's imprecision on this point, central to his analysis is striking. In any case, by 1978 the "local Marwari business houses, representing traders, tea planters and industrialists" too were won over by the Assamese middle classes. This group found the anti-democratic content of the Assam movement pretty "handy". The Marwari big bourgeois elements, one should remember, do not speak Assamese and "were themselves the victims of a racial hate campaign and riots during 1966-68". Yet, they seem to have an indomitable instinct for class suicide. For apart from knowing their vulnerability to a movement of linguistic nationalism, they could also see that there might be only a short leap from blockading oil and plywood to challenging the very structure of capitalist underdevelopment in Assam. Indeed, it should not be surprising if the Assam movement had sent jitters across the tea, plywood and oil establishments with interests in Assam.

Guha's narration of the conjunctural crisis of the Assamese dominant classes reads more like an invention growing out of his theoretical necessity rather than a real crisis produced by peasant or working class militancy. To anyone familiar with the crisis of backward capitalism in India and the death throes of a raw material producing periphery like Assam as well as the recurrent expressions of the unsolved nationality questions in the area, a wave of populist sub-nationalism should not come as a surprise. Six years ago a perceptive correspondent from Guwahati concluded his report with a prophetic observation: The picture, all in all, is a gloomy one. Guwahati is slowly evolving into a typical Indian 'city'; that is, little enclaves of opulence and splendour surrounded by the most abject and degrading kind of poverty and filth. . . . In areas which were till the other day part of Assam, insurgency is going on, and the whole might of the Indian Army is powerless to suppress the national aspirations of small communities. Failing to crush the insurgency, the Indian Army tries to wage a war against a whole people, practice terror. And yet, hardly a ripple of the events in Mizoram and Nagaland seems to have been felt in Assam. But one's impressions might be wrong, and tomorrow might yet be another[7].

That in the event of a nationality upsurge in Assam, leftists might find themselves on the wrong side of the barricade even without "proto-fascist" conspiracies is also not unexpected. Writing long before the anti-foreigners' movement had begun, Bhabani Sengupta had observed : "Not merely the Marxists, but the left movement generally, has been crippled by the nationality question which, in Assam, boils down to the attritious relations between the Assamese and Bengali-speaking people"[8].

One wonders why people who are well conversant with Assam were taken so much by surprise by the Assam movement that they had to invent foreign conspiracies and sudden crisis of Assamese dominant classes to explain the movement. To those who were hoping that a populist mobilization could be pre-empted by the electoral victory for a left front which could then join the historic battle for a change in Centre-state relations, the Assam events might be a little disappointing. Their way of addressing the problem of uneven capitalist development might be more elegant than the untidy course of a mass movement. But history cannot be expected to proceed along the neat trajectories of party political programmes. Why Assam's sub-nationalist upsurge occurred in 1979 and not in 1975 is the wrong question to ask for anyone who grants politics and nationality questions their autonomy. But for someone who sets out to locate political phenomena in precise class demands and conjunctural crisis it is an important question which is left unanswered. On the whole, Guha's argument is made too sloppily to be convincing to anyone who does not accept on faith any party line on Assam.

PLURAL SOCIETY

Guha reserves his harshest criticism for my use of the concept of plural society. The concept, he claims, is "borrowed from neo-colonial social scientists - Chicago sociologists and Cambridge historians, for example, who attempt to deny usefulness of such categories as class and nationalism in the case of third world countries like India". My short articles, written under the pressure of events, clearly left room for some misunderstanding. One wishes, however, that before launching such a tirade, Guha had looked more carefully into the intellectual history of the concept.

The origins of the concept lie in a book by J.S. Furnivall published in 1939[9]. An economic historian of the Dutch colonies of South-east Asia Furnivall focused on the fact that the colonial societies are segmented into two or more ethnic or racial groups. The formulation challenged dominant imperialist ideologies which sought to legitimize the presence of colonial settlers in the colonies, by portraying them as legitimate members of the colonial societies. In the 1960s and 1970s, several scholars extended the concept to other types of societies, made up of more than one ethnic group and not fully sharing a normative consensus. In the classic colonial societies as well as in the case of South Africa, the non-voluntary character of the societies showed up in the use of regulation by force in other situations where the concept has been applied, such as Belgium, Northern Ireland, British West Indies or Lebanon, the defining element is the centrality of a political arrangement between community leaders for the cohesion of the societies. The rationale for such a concept was aptly given by M.G. Smith in his study of the British West Indies: "It is purely Pickwickian to assert that since 'no society can exist without a minimum sharing of common values', societies based on conquest, slavery or colonial domination must inevitably possess these common values, since they clearly exist... the central issue is the presence or absence of such normative consensus between these strata"[10]. The concept is neither used exclusively in the context of third world countries, nor is it applicable to all such countries. I have used it as a conceptual tool to understand Assam's society and polity, which has been based on exceptional immigration. Nowhere have I implied that the concept is an alternative to class analysis or to the notion of a multinational India, as Guha contends.

Guha has faith in the process of assimilation. The evolution of neo-Assamese dialects such as *Saadri or Garden-baat* are persuasive evidence on the trends towards assimilation. Much less convincing, however, is the Census data, as evidence for assimilation. Only empirical studies, which are lacking at this stage, can shed light on the real extent of assimilation. Guha rightly observes: "To say that there has been no real assimilation in Assamese society is as much a half-truth as saying that assimilation is complete." His faith in assimilation however becomes a constraint to a dispassionate examination of all the evidence. The recurring language riots in Assam are seen not as an important aspect of the conflict-ridden Assamese society, but as "anti-minority pogroms" halting the trend of assimilation. Guha's description can be more generously described as the exaggeration of a well-meaning believer in assimilation, distressed by the instances of conflict. Pious thoughts, however, have not been the hallmark of good social science. That Guha himself has found it necessary to distinguish between 'Asamiya' and the 'Assamese' illustrates the need for a plural society type of formulation. To me the fact that the Asamiyas had a nationality upsurge of an unprecedented scale involving nearly the entire Asamiya civil society, but excluding by its very logic the Bengalis - who on their part could bring out lakhs of people to the streets to oppose the Asamiya upsurge - calls for serious analysis. Those on the receiving end of the so-called 'anti-minority pogroms', unlike victims of 'pogroms' anywhere else, have in Assam carried out their own versions of 'pogroms' under the benign cover of minority rights. That aspect of Assam's violence unfortunately continues to need emphasis given the one sided picture presented by people like Guha. Thus, the correspondent for *Mainstream* after a tour of the rural areas of the Nowgong district in June 1980 reported that, "by and large in Nowgong area the Assamese were at the receiving end of the violence unleashed by the counter-agitation", though "some immigrant Muslim families living in the Assamese majority villages were also attacked". He quotes many instances of "immigrants armed with spears and knives" attacking Assamese villages. At Mohirabari for example, "sixteen houses were burnt and three Assamese were killed. There were still a large number of Assamese missing. Every other day a body is found floating in the Brahmaputra."[11] These instances of conflict are more than just irritants in the process of assimilation. The concept of plural society attempts to come to grips with this peculiarity of the Assamese society.

Fortunately, politicians in Assam have an intuitive understanding of the Assamese plural society. They do not resort to pretensions. Thus, during the Parliamentary election campaign of 1977, Devkanta Barooah told members of his Congress party: "When you have the Alis (immigrant Bengali Muslims) and the coolies (tea-garden workers), why should you be afraid of the others?" The attitude summaries the predicament of Assam's basic population. Fakhruddin Ali Ahmed, Assam's best known migrant politician* never learnt to speak the local language fluently. That however did not prove to be a hurdle to his career as a people's representative. In 1975 Ali Ahmed's visit to Assam was the occasion for an interesting piece of reporting: "The President of India visited his 'home state' for the first time since becoming President, and for four days early this month, it looked as if nothing mattered except the Presidential visit. The expression 'home state' is put in inverted commas, for even though now avidly claimed by one and all as Assamese. Fakhruddin Ali Ahmed is not exactly the rigueur. But he has been forgiven the constant lapses in accent and syntax."[12] To many, Ali Ahmed's language might seem to be the epitome of assimilation. The present Assam cabinet might provide more interesting examples of such linguistic assimilation. If a collaborating local elite in the past had forgiven these leaders, the lapses in grammar and in protecting the nation's borders, social scientists would do well to exercise caution before heralding such linguistic monstrosities as evidence of assimilation.

ON LEFT STRATEGY

Eric Hobsbawm in a recent article has reminded Marxists of Lenin's warning to Zinoviev at the Baku Congress of 1920: "Do not paint nationalism red." There is a danger that Marxists might be tempted to "welcome nationalism as ideology and programme rather than realistically to accept it as a fact, a condition of their struggle as socialists". The test, continues Hobsbawm, "must be the Marxist's own country or people"[13]. In my articles, I had stressed the need "to accept Assamese sub-nationalism as real" and to go beyond the slanders of patriots and traitors. Unfortunately, those holding the dominant left view on Assam have systematically tried to portray all dissenting left opinion as Assamese nationalism. It is conveniently forgotten however that on the Assam issue, it is not just Assamese nationalism which might inhibit correct analysis. The near-consensus on Assam across the political spectrum in West Bengal - with some former CPI (ML) groups as a significant exception - should make any objective left observer feel uncomfortable. Assamese nationalists could be forgiven for not always being able to distinguish between a certain left tendency and Bengali nationalism. Such confusions are bound to persist so long as those living in nationalist glass-houses continue throwing stones.

In vulgar Marxism, all non-economic levels of social reality appear as epiphenomena reducible to the economic base. Recent Marxist theories on the relative autonomy of politics and ideology make a decisive break from economism. Whatever else it might mean, the notion of relative autonomy in the context of the nationality question must grant that nationalities have fears and aspirations not reducible to the interests of this or that class. One does not have to deny, however, that different classes play greater or lesser roles in the formation of nationalities or that most nationality upsurges occur within the hegemony of bourgeois ideology.

Nationalist political interventions mostly do not challenge bourgeois property relations any more than a programme of turning a few sharecroppers into surplus-producing farmers challenge the hegemony of the bourgeoisie. But nationalist political interventions do not in themselves, have a determinate class content. The historical association of the Assamese people with the eco-system of the Brahmaputra valley has produced a set of powerful historical and cultural symbols linking the people with 'their' territory. Nationalities do not have rights in a vacuum. Their linguistic and cultural rights have to operate in particular territories. It is in recognition of the association of nationalities with particular territories that the principle of linguistic states has been accepted in India. In themselves the symbols of an eco-system are class natural. They are the raw material for populist mobilization. But when in times of systemic crisis radical forces make history, they make it not in confrontation with these symbols. The left in these moments have these symbols on their side. If the left in Assam today pretend that they are believers in class mobilization and natural opponents of the symbols of Assamese nationalism, they only attempt to cover up their present political ineffectiveness. This view would be a poor guide to future political action.

There can be little doubt that the programme of the Assam movement is not something that the left could become wildly enthusiastic about. In my first article itself I had noted that taking Assamese sub-nationalism seriously does not mean that Marxists and progressives should support the programme of the Assam movement. A programme of detection, deletion and deportation of foreigners can indeed put the fundamental rights of a major segment of Assam's population in jeopardy. That however in itself cannot be an argument for opposing such a programme. If the programme is in principle valid, it can only be an argument for extreme caution in implementation. Historically sensitive analysts would recognize that the demands of protest movements are not always a matter of free choice. The AASU programme did not grow out of thin air. The long history of immigration, illegal infiltration in the post-independence period, the constitutional silence on the means of protecting the historically evolved cultural character of our states and union territories and the support for infiltration from self-seeking politicians had created a situation which led to the Assam upsurge. An element of what Guha calls a 'negative programme' of deportation or re-settlement is perhaps indispensable today if the rights of Assam's basic population have to be protected. This has been recognized by all political parties in so far as they have accepted the demand of deporting the post-1971 infiltrators. The major component of a solution, however, should include steps such as re-organization of Assam and constitutional measures for protecting the rights of Assam's basic population in future. There are precedents of such protective measures in Jammu and Kashmir and in the 'tribal' majority states such as Meghalaya, Arunachal Pradesh and Nagaland. The left can take the initiative in formulating a positive programme.

The left needs to critically examine their perspectives and their strategies in relation to Assam, the north-east and other areas where the nationality question has cropped up. First, has the left done enough to articulate the cultural demands of vulnerable nationalities? Second, has it adequately fought for the specific economic demands of these backward areas? Guha thinks that the left achievements in Assam on this account are laudable. He says that economic underdevelopment has been one of the "basic points of the agitation and propaganda communists of all shades have been carrying on in Assam since independence". The CPI (M) MP, Jyotirmoy Basu, he reminds us "used the floor of Parliament to give voice to the agonies of Assam". This, however, is a rather complacent view of left accomplishments. Let us take one example, Assam's integration into the capitalist economy as a tea-producing area is a major factor in Assam's present underdevelopment. Tea occupies 15,000,000 acres of Assam's best agricultural lands. The industry, which covers up its super-profits by systematically manipulating books, has made little contribution to the general development of the area. British companies continue to be dominant in tea. Today nationalization of tea is a necessary condition for Assam's development. As a classic colonial primary commodity, tea is hardly a technologically intensive sector which can claim exemption from the Foreign Exchange Regulation Act (FERA). Indeed, it is nothing short of a scandal that non-resident share-holders in Indianised tea companies are allowed to have 74 per cent of the equity capital as against the FERA norm of maximum of 40 per cent in other industries. While the left is not responsible for the decision, the persistence of foreign control in tea surely does not speak too high of its record.

Major segments of the left have understood the Assam movement in terms of the actions of a few leaders and a chauvinist local press. Some journalists, sympathetic to the movement, have portrayed the student leaders as heroes. Others in the left have portrayed them as villains. The government's attempt at solving the Assam problem through press censorship and selective repression flows directly from such a superficial, a historical understanding. Such measures predictably have not brought us any closer to the solution. The mass mobilization during the Assam movement has become possible because of the history of the Assamese perception, whether one agrees with it or not, is complex. There is considerable ambiguity and anguish within it. But such anguish and dilemma can easily be swept aside in vulgar Marxist analysis of the Assam events.

[I wish to thank Manju Purikh, Rahul Bose and Swapan Dasgupta for their comments which helped clarify some of the points made in the paper. The responsibility for the arguments, of course, is entirely mine].

REFERENCES

1. Since Guha's earlier articles on the Assam movement published elsewhere have not been discussed, it is not implied that Guha has retreated from his earlier positions. The retreat and concession is not Guha's own previous position, but the positions

taken by the political tendency that Guha represents.

2. V.I. Lenin, "The Question of Nationalities or 'Autonomisation'", (notes written on December 21, 1922), reprinted in Lenin, "The Liberation Movement in the East", Moscow, 1969, p. 327.
3. The term 'basic population' appears in M.I. Isayev, "National Language in the USSR", Moscow, 1977. He uses the term to mean the "peoples that have given their names to the republics or autonomous regions"; See p. 349-50.
4. V.I. Lenin, The Discussion on Self-Determination Summed Up' written in July 1916, reprinted in Lenin, *op. cit.*, p. 193. Lenin incidentally was referring to the Zimmerwald group's attempt to belittle the Irish rebellion of 1916 by calling it a putsch, which it was alleged, a "purely urban, petty bourgeois movement, which, notwithstanding the sensation it caused, had not much social backing". Lenin found the assessment "monstrously doctrinaire and pedantic".
5. Susanta Krishna Dass, 'Stalemate in Assam-II', *The Statesman,* Calcutta, December 31,1980.
6. This and the following points are based on Ernesto Laclau. 'Fascism and Ideology', in "Politics and Ideology in Marxist Theory", London, 1977.
7. M.S. Prabhakar, "Assam: Visitations", *EPW,* February 22, 1975.
8. Bhabani Sengupta, The CPI (M), p. 195.
9. J.S. Furniall, "Netherlands India: A Study of Plural Economy", Cambridge, 1939.
10. M.G. Smith, "The Plural Society of the British West Indies", 1965. p. xi.
11. Ghanshyam Pardesi, *Mainstream,* June 28,1980.

* Fakhruddin Ali Ahmed was not an immigrant. His ancestral home is at Kacharihat, now Golaghat district of Assam where his father Dr. Col., Jalnur AH, a military doctor, was born. Ali Ahmed was born at Gonda, Uttar Pradesh. Ali Ahmed was brought up outside Assam because of his father's nature of job. He came to Assam in 1935 to join the legal profession at Guwahati. Further, his mother was an Urdu speaking person. Naturally, he could not speak Assamese fluently - Editor.

12. M.S. Prabhakar, *op cit.*
13. Eric Hobsbawm, "Some Reflections on 'The Break-up of Britain", *New Left Review,* Sept-Oct, 1977.

12

Little Nationalism Turned Chauvinist
A Reply*

—Antalendu Guha

In his 8-point critique *(EPW,* February 21) Udayon Misra evades discussion on the basic issues I raised in my original article. He concentrates his fire, on the contrary, on some minor points, not of much significance for upholding or demolishing my stand.

From a Marxist-Leninist point of view, the solution of Assam's foreigner issue lies, I had argued, not in putting the clock back by thirty years or so, but (i) in an emphasis, largely, on assimilation of all the pre-1971 immigrants; (ii) in calling for a halt to further immigration across the international frontiers; and (iii) an extension of autonomy. In my article, the pre-1917 Ukrainian and Russian experience was cited and Lenin was quoted at length in support of such a policy of assimilation. The demand for deportation and d is enfranchisement of hundreds and thousands of post 1951 settlers - almost all of them toiling people, indiscriminately

* *EPW,* Vol. XVI, No. 17, April 25, 1981, pp. 781-84.

called foreigners by the chauvinist movement - was said to be undemocratic and reactionary. Did not Lenin pinpoint "the historically progressive nature of the assimilation of the Great Russian and Ukrainian" while dealing with a largely similar anti-foreigner movement in pre-Revolutionary Ukraine?

To all this, Misra turns a deaf ear. His critique steers clear of any reference to Lenin's teachings - and for that matter also to Mao's - on the national question in general and on the backlog of immigration from a neighbouring area in particular. Instead, he tries to pick holes in the data-base of my article and deplores my "total silence" on another issue - the Congress (I) Government's repression that followed the chauvinist movement. Let me reply to Misra's serially numbered comments in the same order.

It is unfair on Misra's part to charge me with "concealing the fact that till 1874 Sylhet was never a part of Assam". How could the question of concealment arise, and for what purpose? How could a well-known historical fact be concealed at all? Not only in my book on Assam, but also in section I (p 1699) of my aforesaid article, it was indicated that Sylhet, not being a part of the erstwhile Ahom state, was not included in the Assam Division of the Bengal Presidency during 1826-1873 and that the Bengali-speaking districts were joined to this Division in 1874 to form the new Province of Assam. To say that I "give sole credit to the Asamiya middle class chauvinists for the separation of Sylhet from Assam" in 1947 is also a distortion of truth. Not only in my book, but also in section I of my article, it was clearly stated that the Congress committees of both the Assam and Surma (Sylhet/Cachar) Valleys "were by and large, able to stand together on the Sylhet question till 1946" and that "the Congress stood for separation of Sylhet from Assam" (pp 1704-5). Hence, there could be no question of my saying that the demand for the separation of Sylhet during 1874-1946 was exclusively a demand of the Asamiya middle class chauvinists. Rather, I have always highlighted the legitimacy of the demand. Misra should not have read too much in the expression "Sylhet was shaken off its back". It simply means that while the Asamiya middle class, by and large, continued its efforts to get Sylhet out of Assam until the goal was achieved, its Bengali counterpart in Sylhet shifted its position after 1946 and largely worked against the proposed secession of Sylhet during the Sylhet Referendum of July 1947. All this should have been known to Misra had he read my book and article more carefully.

II

"According to Guha, the Bengali-speaking population in reconstituted post-1947 Assam declined from 30 per cent in 1931 to 21 per cent in 1951 and 20 per cent in 1971. While referring to this sharp decline in the post-1947 period, Guha should have mentioned that the chief reason behind this was the separation of Sylhet - the most populous Bengali-speaking district from Assam". This kind of misreading on Misra's part is unwarranted and unfortunate. For, what I had said on p 1710 in section III of my article was : ". . . with its share in the total population *of reconstituted Assam of today,* steadily declining from 30 per cent in 1931 to 21 per cent in 1951" (emphasis added). Clearly, my 1931 figure stands for reconstituted Assam, as of today, and does not cover Sylhet area that was later transferred to Pakistan. Had Sylhet been included in the 1931 coverage, Bengali-speakers' share in Assam's total population would have been given as no less than 40 per cent. In fact, I have said so in so many words also in Section I, p. 1701: "Later, during 1874-1947, it used to form part of a separate Province . . . in which Asamiya was the claimed mother tongue of less than a quarter and Bengali of more than 40 per cent of the population".

Misra also doubts the fact that, as per census records, the Asamiya-speaking population increased 80 per cent and the Bengali-speaking population 71 per cent during the 1951-71 period. The same data, when tabulated decade-wise, "gives a different picture", according to him. No doubt, Assam's Bengali-speaking population increased 20 per cent during 1951-61 and

41 per cent during 1961-71, as against Asamiya-speaking population's growth of 36 and 31 per cent, respectively. But these figures do not falsify the 20 years period average growth rates. As there was no language census for 1941 and as we are interested in long-run trends, a 20-year periodisation (1931-51 and 1951-71) was found more useful. Besides, the whole controversy over the foreigner issue is limited to the 1951-1971 period. So, we tried to find out whether, because of migration, the Assamese society of 1971 became linguistically different and culturally less viable than that of 1951. The relevant growth rates, simultaneously influenced by three determinants - (i) natural population growth, (ii) population growth by way of net migration and (iii) population growth by way of linguistic conversion - were found in no way unfavourable to the cause of preservation of the Asamiya identity. It now appears that the whole exercise has fallen flat on Misra.

III

Misra's other serious charge is that I quoted Tarunram Phukan "out of context" and that, too, with a wrong translation. It is possible that the Asamiya word, *Prabhaba,* would have been better translated as 'dominance', rather than as 'domination'. But even after such a change, the meaning would have remained, given the context, substantially the same. If the "sign of life of a rising nationality", according to Phukan, was "to extend dominance (or 'influence' as Misra suggests) over others", then his nationalism had certainly also a regional dimension and an aggressive tone as well. As the quoted text of his address reveals, he was aggrieved to find the Asamiyas incapable of extending such influence/dominance over other nationalities and, instead, even a dependent neighbour was "trying to swallow us". I quoted from Phukan not to prove that he was a little nationalist of the chauvinist brand, but to show that even he, a man with an all-India outlook, was at times affected by what was bad in the Asamiya little nationalism. Despite this lapse and other lapses like his proving himself a renegade to the Congress and its civil disobedience movement in the 1930s, my assessment of the overall role of Tarunram Phukan has always been positive.

IV

Nationalism is a spiritual sentiment as well as an ideology that, irrespectively of its class roots, reaches out to the peasantry and thus may attain a mass character. Nationalism is democratic and progressive to the extent it aims at drawing the peasant into a wider national market by freeing him from feudal ties and culture. Nationalism is reactionary, if its impact is otherwise. Besides, it can be labeled as peasant nationalism only when the peasants become its driving force, *with an anti-feudal programme.* No such signs are visible in the current anti-foreigner frenzy. Had this frenzy been a case of peasant nationalism, its thrust would have been (at least by and large) against the feudal exploiters including the local landlords and moneylenders and not against the toiling peasants and other settlers of non-Asamiya origin.

Sizeable sections of the peasantry surely joined the frenzy. But this they did because of a myth-fed fear psychosis (that of being turned into a national minority in their own homeland) and also out of age-old racial prejudices against the Bengalis. But that does not make the frenzy justified and respectable.

Misra should have also noted that the immigrants settled down on the wastelands not only in the ryotwari districts, but also in the permanently settled Goalpara district in thousands. The nature of land tenure has little to do with the genesis and character of the anti-foreigner movement, or of the prevailing landlord-tenant relations.

V

Misra, however, raises a pertinent question. If the force of nationalism behind the current anti-foreigner agitation is 'gentry nationalism', how to explain the involvement of some sections of the peasantry, including those of tribal origin? We have already partially answered this. It may be added that acute economic stagnation, with the growing problems of indebtedness, landlessness and unemployment, is at the root of the general discontent. Peasants' discontent and their desire for increased autonomy has been exploited by vested interests and given a chauvinist twist. Ignorant, conservative and backward peasants have been misguided by the rural gentry. Instead of uniting the toilers of all communities, linguistic and religious, in a common anti-feudal, anti-monopoly struggle, the movement has divided them on the basis of communalism and divisive slogans. Even the tribal peasants are now antagonized, since the movement is lukewarm, if not hostile, to their demands for local autonomy in demarcated tribal areas, job reservations, restoration of all transferred lands to their original tribal proprietors and school education through the medium of mother-tongues. Who are more sympathetic to these just demands of the tribal peasantry - the organized platform of the anti-foreigner agitation or the organized left movement? Misra should have dealt with this question.

VI

"Assimilation is a process of interpenetration and fusion in which persons and groups acquire the memories, sentiments, attitudes of other persons or groups and, by sharing their experiences and history, are incorporated with them in a cultural life." [Park and Burgess, *Introduction to the Science of Sociology,* Chicago, 1921, p.735]. Misra has muddled ideas about this ongoing historical process of voluntary integration or assimilation. It is a two-way traffic and does not necessarily involve total linguistic conversion; although that, too, might take place.

In fact, in the Assam context, Asamiyaisation through linguistic conversion is only one form of assimilation. There could be assimilation even without it. While discussing the national question, Lenin pointed out that assimilation in multi-lingual Switzerland was achieved on the basis of equal rights for several languages while, in the United States, it was achieved on the basis of adoption of one common language by diverse national groups. Both the processes were progressive.

Historically, both the processes are active in contemporary Assamese society. In Assam, people whose conditions of life and work make it necessary for them to know the Asamiya language are learning it without being forced to do so, not only as a bazaar tongue, but also as a first or second language at the school level. But coercion and talk of deportation will hinder the Asamiya language "from spreading to other national groups"; most important of all, it will sharpen otherwise reconcilable minor national contradictions.

Just as there are chauvinists among the Asamiyas, so there are chauvinists also among the Bengali-speaking and other minority groups in Assam, who resent and even resist assimilation. Yet the overall long-run trend of the last one hundred years, particularly of the post-independence years, has been undoubtedly one of growing assimilation, even of Asamiyaisation. This is clearly reflected in Assam's census statistics on mother tongues (as I showed in my article) and on bilingualism. For example, in 1961, out of 8,99,000 persons recording Bengali as their mother tongue in the Brahmaputra Valley, 5,34,000 (more than 59 per cent) recorded Asamiya as their second language (relevant figures for 1971 are yet to be received). As against this, less than 4 per cent of the Valley's 67,31,000 Asamiya speakers claimed Bengali as their second language in the same year. All this suggests that the backlog of continued migration till 1971 has in no way endangered the Asamiya language and cultural identity in their own homeland. Marxist-Leninists should take note of this historical trend, and they should help in every way the process of assimilation by fighting chauvinism. The undue fear of being turned into a minority in the long run (when we are all dead) could and should be removed by all means other than inhumanly unsettling lakhs of settled toiling people.

Misra's argument that the Bengalis in Assam, in general, will successfully resist or skip assimilation because they are "part of a distinct developed nationality" or because "they have concentrated themselves in certain 'pockets' in the

Brahmaputra Valley" does not sound Marxist. The assimilation process in both the United States and Switzerland, as pointed out by Lenin, involved parts of such distinct and still more developed nationalities. Yet, were not the Germans, living often in pockets of concentration, assimilated to larger entities in Switzerland and US? I would rather agree with what Birendrakumar Bhattacharya, the doyen of contemporary Asamiya literatures, wrote in 1973: "Geographical and occupational factors will compel or are compelling the Bengalis or other immigrants to adjust themselves to the new cultural environment, an environment that has affected and shaped the growth of Assamese. The compulsions of cultural, political and economic mobilization will also compel different classes of Bengalis in Assam to practise bilingualism in such a manner that the antagonism between the two languages will finally fade away" *(North Eastern Research Bulletin,* Dibrugarh University, Volume 4, 1973).

VII

I plead guilty of both accusing the Asam Sahitya Sabha of "fanning chauvinistic frenzy" and, at the same time, of praising it for its interest in the collection and publication of Mymensinghia folk tales. I wish the Sabha continues its literary activities and disassociates itself totally from the politics of chauvinism (as revealed in its official memoranda and resolutions as pointed out by me) that is dividing the Assamese people and hindering further spread of the Asamiya language among other national groups.

VIII

State violence committed against the people of Assam during the current agitation is surely as bad as violence incited and committed by the latter. Hundreds of people have been killed in the name of the movement; and dozens, in the name of suppressing it. I gathered the impression from a recent visit to Guwahati that the left, including the CPI(M) and the

CPKM-D/SNS group; has not hesitated to denounce all attacks on people's liberties and freedom of movement and expression, no matter whether such attacks came from the government or from the organized platform of the agitation. All defenders of liberty should come forward jointly to denounce all such attacks. It would then begin to thaw, and prospects of an all-party settlement would brighten. I shall give one example as to how the problems come before us in concrete shape. In March 1981, the students were back in their class-rooms to sit for the ensuing examinations. But all v/as not quiet in the Gauhati University campus, the headquarters of the AASU leaders. A number of students, marked for their opposition to the agitation, were disallowed entry into their hostel rooms and were forced to stay either outside the campus or in the University Guest House under threats from the AASU followers. The affected students asked for CRP protection in the absence of any guarantee of their security from the University authorities. On the other hand, the AASU students said they would boycott the examinations in case the CRP entered the campus. In such a tense situation, if the citizens on the campus collectively fail to give protection to the minorities, the CRP becomes acceptable to the latter. This is the tragedy of the situation. After all, the most fundamental of all rights is the right to life.

Or, consider what has happened to Bijanlal Chaudhuri, a college teacher of Asamiya literature and distinguished essayist, who is opposed to the 'anti-foreigner' movement. He and his family have been facing inhuman torture for the last two years. Organised gangs have followed him and hindered his free movement whenever he ventured to go out on the streets of his own home town, Barpeta. Students have been debarred by the agitation leaders from talking to him or attending his classes under threats of dire consequences. Attempts have been made by a Ku Klux Klan-type secret gang to kidnap his son and a bomb was thrown on his house. Above all, the college principal has continued to withhold his pay for all these two years on the plea of his failure to attend the college. It is a pity that 'intellectuals' who miss no opportunity to denounce CRP excesses and government's attacks on citizens' rights remain totally callous to similar attacks on citizens' liberties in the name of sustaining the agitation. The University campus incidents and the treatment meted out to Bijanlal Chaudhuri at Barpeta, for instance, went unprotested by those 'intellectuals' who are with the agitation.

I did make a brief mention of the danger from the rising authoritarianism in my article and I elaborated this point in a subsequent note in *EPW,* February 14, "At this critical juncture in Assam, even basic human rights like the freedom of expression are daily coming under attack from both the chauvinist agitators and bureaucratic authoritarianism. . . . Chauvinism can be defeated in the long run only through persistent ideological and political work, and not by invoking repression by organs of state power from above".

To conclude, ideological and political work does not mean only an exposure of the chauvinist slogans, but also presentation of an alternative programme of increased autonomy for linguistic areas, modified Centre-state relations in favour of the latter, regional economic and cultural development and due protection to all languages and cultures in a way that would remove the fear psychosis of the Asamiya people, in particular and at the same time, would not turn lakhs of settled people homeless. A tripartite round table conference could consider, or work, for such a programme while discussing the settlement of the 'foreigner' issue. At such a level, even the question of separation of Cachar from Assam, as suggested by Sanjib Baruah elsewhere, could be given the consideration it deserves, provided it is acceptable to the anti-foreigner platform.

Now for a brief response to Gail Omvedt's comments *(EPW,* March 28). Assam's problem was indeed posed in my article as a national question, but as one of 'territorial autonomy' for the present, rather than as one of 'self-determination', following Lenin's terminology. It was also pointed out that, even when the right to self-determination (i.e. the right to secession from an exploitative state) is conceded in principle, the proletariat reserves its right to oppose such secession for the sake of larger interests. This is the Leninist position. Even at the risk of being charged with "trading quotations from Lenin", I would like to draw Omvedt's attention to the following guidelines, from the same source (Collected Works, Volume 20, p. 412):

The bourgeois nationalism of any oppressed nation has a general democratic content that is directed against oppression and it is this content that we *unconditionally* support. At the same time, we strictly distinguish it from the tendency towards national exclusiveness, we fight against the tendency of the Polish bourgeois to oppress the Jews, etc.

The left movement has no record of remaining silent on economic, social and cultural oppression carried on against the Assamese people, including the tribals. It did not fail to give due recognition to the problem of unauthorized immigration and to demand more power for the state. It has always consistently fought against the force of "national exclusiveness" and racial prejudices against the Bengalis and the tribals. The left is in agreement with Gail Omvedt when she says that "nationality issues are quite complex" and that "for the left, balancing the needs of different national groups in a single region and giving them an overall revolutionary thrust is never easy". The region needs such a solution as is acceptable not only to major sections of the Asamiya caste Hindus, but also to the tribals and other minorities living in Assam today. I want also to make it clear that I did not mean, even by implication, that "the formation of separate Naga and Mizo states was a chauvinistic mistake", as Omvedt suggests. It was, of course, partly a response to the provocative and narrow-minded policy of the Asamiya chauvinists on language and culture. It is not clear to me whether Omvedt wants more linguistic areas (Cachar, Karbi Anglong, etc.) to be carved out of the present state of Assam. If so, I am afraid, she will create a greater distance between herself and the Asamiya followers of the anti-foreigner movement than what exists between the organized left and the latter. This is the kind of problem the left is facing in the region. Under the circumstances, the maintenance of national peace on a give-and-take basis has a higher priority than bookish slogans.

Yet another point. If we go by the available data on birth-place, mother-tongue, bilingualism, literary activities, field experience, etc., then we can say that the Asamiya cultural identity is not in danger. This is what I said. Such a phrase as "no objective basis for any grievance" should not have been ascribed to me. Assam has a thousand other grievances, as many other states also have. But that is a separate issue.

Omvedt's brief points on the Russian-Ukrainian situation are not convincing. Had Ukraine been a more developed class society than Russia, why did its differentiated peasantry fail to provide the necessary supply to the labour market for its industries (as it happens in Assam)? Who owned most of Ukraine's industries and its lands? These questions have to be answered before we accept such a statement. If the number of mines, oil installation and factories be any criterion of 'development', then the Brahmaputra Valley is surely more developed than Bangladesh (East Bengal). But does that make the Assam situation closer to the Ukrainian situation in terms of Omvedt's logic?

It is also not clear what Omvedt means by the term "a greater Bengali nationality". Does she mean that the Bengalis of Bangladesh, West Bengal and Cachar today form one nationality? Does she also say that the Germans of Switzerland, Germany and Austria form, in the same way, one nationality? If so, I have fundamental difference with her.

Gail Omvedt should answer straight whether the left and democratic forces of Assam could afford to support a platform that demands deportation of lakhs of toiling people, settled in their present habitat for the last ten to thirty years. The fact that the left and their allies agreed to the principle of unsettling all those who had come after 1971 suggests that they did care for the sentiments of the Asamiya masses, since those sentiments - however unfounded and cruel - had become a part of the reality we face today. In practice, the left has committed many mistakes in its attempts to resolve the national question over the years. For more than five years beginning 1946, it held the same views, as Omvedt holds today, on such questions as self-determination and the right to secede. As it gathered greater experience of the Indian reality, it abandoned its mechanical understanding of the national question. It is hoped that Omvedt also will get cured of the infantile disorder she is suffering from.

13

Little Nationalism Turned Chauvinist
A Summing Up*

—*Amalendu Guha*

In continuation of my reply to Gail Omvedt *(EPW,* April 25), I may inform that the left's concern for Assam's acute underdevelopment and immigration problems goes back much beyond November 1980 and is, in no way, a by-product of "pressure from the movement". As demanded by her, some relevant facts of the post-independence period regarding "what the CPI and CPI(M) were saying about the issue years earlier" are presented below in Section I. Sanjib Baruah's comment *(EPW,* April 11) is examined in Section II. My final position, in its immediate operational aspects, is restated in Section III.

I

Early in 1947, the Assam Provincial Organising Committee, CPI, published in Asamiya a pamphlet under the title 'Communist Party's Call or Halting the Immigrants'

---

* *EPW,* Vol. XVI, No. 21, May 23, 1981, pp. 957-64.

Influx and Saving Assam from an Impending Civil Strife'. It pointed out that such an influx, if unrestrained, would endanger "the very national existence" of the Assamese people'[1]. The first conference of the same committee, held at Gauhati on February 11-14, 1948, passed a resolution on "the land settlement and eviction in Assam". Amongst other things, it said: "The very question of self-existence of the Assamese people as a distinct and growing nationality now hinges on this point arid, naturally enough, the people of Assam are seriously perturbed with an intense desire for checking further immigration"[2]. This resolution appears to have remained a general guideline for the left of all shades in Assam. For instance, Phani Bora, a leader of the CPI, told the Assam Legislative Assembly in 1967 that corrupt government officials were helping trans-frontier infiltration into Assam and that the ruling party welcomed it with a view to creating a vote bank. "I am for driving out Pakistani infiltrators and other foreigners; but for that", he said, "let the law take its own course"[3]. Incidentally, the CPI (M) had no representation in the Assam Legislative Assembly until 1978. Besides, no party or organization - not even the Asam Sahitya Sabha - had till then demanded deportation of all post-1951 settlers of East Bengal origin with retrospective effect. In no way could the left be held responsible for the influx of population that had taken place in the past. For neither at the Union nor at the state level did they wield power or formulate public policies.

Since their first participation in 1952, communist legislators had incessantly raised demands, *inter alia,* also for a tea auction market at Guwahati, broad gauge railways, bridges over the Brahmaputra, oil refineries, shifting of the registered headquarters of all Assam based joint-stock companies from Calcutta to Guwahati, nationalization of select industries and increased powers for the state government. It was, primarily, under the leadership of the CPI and the then Praja Socialist Party that the first oil refinery movement had attained a mass character and forced the Centre to build a refinery in Assam by 1962. It was again the

Sibsagar Zila Parishad of the CPI that first voiced the demand for a second oil refinery. This triggered off another state-wide mass movement which, however, came to be dominated by anti-communist chauvinist elements. For, after their historic split, the communists in Assam had temporarily lost much of the effectiveness, the united CPI had on the earlier occasion.

Even as late as 1972, the CPI (M) was an insignificant political force in Assam, as can be gauged from the following figures published in a party source[4].

Party Membership (1972)	1,188
CITU Membership (1971)	2,529
SFI Membership (1971)	2,000
Kisan Front Members (1971)	18,094

It was through a continuous and doubledged struggle against the forces of big and small nationality chauvinisms that the CPI (M) and other left forces had to advance to their present position of having one-tenth of the state's voters with them. The CPI (M)'s membership and mass base expanded considerably only during Emergency and thereafter.

On September 21, 1978, that is, nearly a year before the AASU formally launched the so-called anti-foreigner movement, the Assam State Committee of the CPI (M) revived the old demands for a halt to further unlawful immigration and additional measures for tightening border security[5]. Reacting as Chief Minister of West Bengal to the Assam agitation, Jyoti Basu in November 1979 considered the "fear of Assamese about outsiders" as "genuine and real"[6]. The CPI (M), Assam State Committee's memorandum submitted to the Union Home Minister on November 30,1979 also referred to "the Asamiya masses' undoubted support to the movement" and their "genuine fear of being politically and culturally endangered under pressure of the non-Asamiya population"[7]. The committee demanded a solution of the problem without undue harassments to the state's minority national groups. All these facts do not suggest that the left, in the past, had remained unconcerned about Assam's predicaments.

The present stand of the left is quite in tune with the earlier CPI resolutions on the issue, as cited above. The CPI (ML), the SUCI and other left democratic forces joined the CPI (M) in issuing on November 17, 1979 a joint appeal at the state level, paying thereby due attention to the Assamese people's anxieties and, at the same time, pointing towards some negative features of the so-called anti-foreigner agitation. They said: "There exists a wide and legitimate concern among the masses for a solution as speedy as possible of this problem of foreign citizens; and this, in the interest of the state and the country at large"[8]. They all agree in principle that 'foreigners' have to be identified on the basis of an agreed definition of the term in constitutional terms, before any attempt for deportation was made. They look forward to a settlement balancing the needs of different national groups. That is why, while warning against conspiracies abroad for dividing the Indian people and secessionism at home, the Central Committee of the CPI (M), in a resolution, dated February 7, 1980, expressed its concern over the "just grievances against the influx of foreign immigrants", as well as the possibility of "their cultural and political identity being in danger"[9]. It appears to welcome any democratic solution that would remove this danger. The CPI (M) and other left parties might have committed many mistakes but apparently none, by identifying the AASU-AAGSP platform as a chauvinist and reactionary one, judging it in terms of its own programme and slogans.

The left's failure to stem the post-1978 tide of chauvinism in Assam is to be linked not to an ideological weakness on the national question, but to the complexity of the situation and their organisational shortcomings; not to their broad strategy, but perhaps to their day-to-day tactics. Their stand of simultaneously fighting both the big and small nationality chauvinisms evolving through a long experience - an experience not yet analysed properly for the benefit of our young radical scholars. The concepts of India's multinationality, national-territorial autonomy and the principle of the right of self-determination have a history.

Though not totally free from mistakes in application even after the withdrawal of the CPI's indiscreet pro-Pakistan stance, this concept remained, on the whole, on or, nearer, correct lines since 1946. A brief outline of the CPI-CPI (M)'s understanding of the national question with reference to Assam in particular is given below.

During 1946-64, this understanding was much similar to Gail Omvedt's current stand, even to the extent of mechanically grafting the right of secession on the Indian situation. Take, for instance, the main political resolution of the first conference of the Assam Committee, CPI, in 1948. It demanded reorganisation of the Province on the basis of its linguistic and geographical features; legal protection of the minority rights, including the right to receive education through mother-tongue at all stages (as far as practicable) and above all, "full provincial autonomy" with a constitutional right to secede from the Indian Union[10].

At the national level, the clause recognizing "the right of all nationalities to self-determination" was there in the CPI Party Programme until its 1964 split. However, in the larger anti-imperialist interests of the Indian proletariat, the party was opposed to the actual exercise of this right in the specific situations of Nagaland, Mizoram, Tamil Nadu and Kashmir, given the international situation. The Seventh Congress of the CPI (M), while adopting a new Programme at Calcutta in 1964, found the aforesaid clause redundant and decided to withhold it until the formulation of a suitably revised stand. The clause was finally dropped from its Programme at its Ninth Congress at Madurai in July 1972 in view of "the danger of different linguistic contingents of the Indian proletariat acquiescing in the secessionist agitations, instead of opposing them and unitedly fighting for real autonomy of states and against any traces of inequality"[11].

Even the People's Democratic Party, Assam, - a DMK-type regional party founded by a communist renegade to fight for Assam's regional interests during the late 1960s and early 1970s - was sober enough not to demand the right to secede or a wholesale deportation of the post 1951 settlers[12]. It raised such demands as autonomy with residual powers lying with the constituent states, equal representation of all states in the Rajya Sabha, creation of autonomous cultural areas within the states and an extension of representative government down to the village level to replace the bureaucratic rule. Incidentally, the CPI (M) and several other left parties also had long stood for these very demands as elements of a consistent democracy, as they still do. After an unsuccessful career, this People's Democratic Party went into voluntary liquidation to merge with the Janata party when the latter was formed. This was the reality in Assam till 1978. In that year the Jatiyatabadi and Purbanchaliya chauvinists failed miserably to emerge even as an oppositional electoral force. Their candidates forfeited deposits while the left secured an unprecedented electoral success, though limited to only 11 per cent of the total votes cast.

It is such a policy on the national question, as explained above, that helped the left - and the CPI (M) in particular -to increase their strength amongst the Asamiya/Assamese toilers over the post-Independence years. Though now temporarily cornered, this strength appears to have undergone greater consolidation in their pockets of influence during the current agitation and counter-agitation. In the Brahmaputra Valley, an overwhelming majority of the members of both the CPI and CPI (M) today are reportedly Asamiya and Bodo by ethnicity and not Bengali, as it used to be before and during the 1950s. The left parties, by and large, did not vacillate under the impact of the rising forces of chauvinism. They refused to support the undemocratic and reactionary platforms of both the AASU and the AAGSP as well as the AAMSU. Theirs was a mission to balance the needs of different national groups with a view to building a common platform. They believe in law- fully preventing the foreigners from border-crossing, rather than hounding out people who are no longer foreigners, but are naturalized citizens in their own right on the basis of long permitted residence for the last ten years or more. It is inhuman and criminal to ask a person to leave the country without proving that he is a foreigner and intruder.

In the given context, a vigorous policy of preventing further immigration with retrospective effect from 1971 or some such proximate date, coupled with a policy of encouraging assimilation and extending autonomy, should suffice to preserve the basic national character of the state of Assam of today. For we see that even as late as 1971, speakers of indigenous languages accounted for about 80 per cent of the population of the Brahmaputra Valley. If 'developed' Ukrainians and 'less developed' Russians could be advised assimilation while still retaining their separate linguistic identities following the Swiss mode in pre-revolutionary Ukraine, there is no reason why 'developed' ethnic Bengalis, 'less developed' Asamiyas and still less developed Bodos cannot be given the same advice. Besides, Omvedt's pessimism about the prospects of'assimilation' (as Lenin understood the term) would have gained weight had she discussed her points fully. Were the Russians less developed also in respect of culture and literature? Could the relatively more developed Asamiyas and relatively less developed Bodos share a common state and assimilate to each other? These are the questions that remain unanswered in the Omvedt-Misra theory of 'development' creating (in some cases) an irremovable hindrance to assimilation. Lenin's theory was different. He argued that with economic development, ethnic resistance to assimilation, or voluntary integration, tended to disappear, as it happened in Switzerland and United States. The national question arises out of general (and not just relative) backwardness and, if left unsolved, hinders progress. To accept such a statement is not to deny that some vestiges of the question might sill survive in advanced countries, but only as vestiges.

The basic solution, therefore, is linked with economic and political development within the frame of a 'consistent democracy'. What is needed to achieve this in Assam or elsewhere is a united struggle of the toiling and oppressed peoples of all national groups against the big bourgeois-landlord rule. Such a struggle will promote assimilation and help resolve the national question on a give-and-take basis. A solution of the national question and achievement of national peace will in turn help the struggle itself for an advance towards socialism.

Omvedt's difficulties in grasping the problem lie not so much in her lack of acquaintance with the Assam situation and her background, as in her reluctance to do homework on relevant documents as are available in published form, before passing casual judgments on the left movement. A relevant portion of the "Note Submitted to the National Integration Council" by P. Sundarayya in October 1973, summarizing his party's stand in the national question, is reproduced below for her consideration:

> The Government which at first refused to recognize the autonomy of Nagaland, Meghalaya, Mizoram, Manipur and Arunachal and take steps to meet their economic, cultural and political aspirations, and bring harmonious development within the state of Assam, has been ultimately forced to make those areas separate states in the Indian Union.
>
> Even now the question of Mikir Hills (now, Karbi Anglong) and the North Cachar Hills district, the question of Cachar district (Bengali-speaking district) within Assam state, are all looming large. The Plain Tribal people (Bodo and other tribal people in the Assam plains), because their just and democratic linguistic and economic demands are not conceded and safeguarded, are raising slogans of separate Statehood, however implausible that may be .....
>
> The legitimate desire of the Assamese-speaking people to make their language the predominant factor in their life, as the medium of education and administration has to be respected. Their fears that Bengali-speaking people would dominate their State should also be removed. If the Assamese-speaking majority and their leaders refuse to concede the democratic rights of linguistic minorities in the State, then these areas where another language-

speaking people are in majority may have to be constituted as separate units outside Assam State. Though the linguistic minorities in the State will be reduced to the minimum, yet the problem of their linguistic rights will continue and these must be safeguarded and guaranteed by the Central Government."[13]

The same note also pressed for the recognition of the Nepal! language on par with other Indian languages in the Eighth Schedule of the Constitution and extended support to the "just demand that Nepalese-speaking tracts be constituted as a separate district in West Bengal with special status". It also voiced the demand for recognizing "Equality of all national languages in Parliament and Central Administration and equality of all the constituent states in the matter of decision-making at the national level by way of reforming the state structure[14]. The tragedy of Tripura - its being transformed from tribal territory into a Bengali-majority one - was no creation of the CPI-CPI (M). The latter continued to protest against the relevant ruling class policies and put forward the demand for the Sixth Schedule autonomy for what could still be salvaged as consolidated reserved tribal areas in Tripura. Bypassing the Centre's refusal to concede and in the face of fierce opposition from Bengali chauvinists, the Left Front Government of Tripura passed an Act to create an autonomous tribal area in the state where, amongst other things, all recently transferred lands were also to be restored to their original tribal owners. It is left-dominated West Bengal, again, that remains the first and so far the only State to have given official recognition to the Santali script, *Olchiki* - a symbol of Santal little nationalism of eastern India.

Will Gail Omvedt spell out in concrete terms - not in piecemeal fashion, but with reference also to the tribal and caste aspirations as well as the much-desired "overall revolutionary thrust" - what other alternative policy could have been suggested for "balancing the needs of different national groups", in north-east India without compromising one's notion of equality, democracy and working-class unity or without inviting Lebanon-type civil strifes?

II

Though loaded with ethnic and anti-left prejudices, the movement, in my view expresses also an urge for autonomy and, unless what is just in it and Assam's injured feelings are attended to, it might end up as secessionist. In fact, secessionist forces are already at work outside and within the movement. Autonomy, as understood by Lenin in a multinational context, is a political reform that may or may not lead to a serious demand for secession, depending on the conjunctural historical circumstances. The fear of loss of identity due to immigration, a recurring theme since about 1920 in Assam, is, indeed, linked with the question of autonomy.

Sanjib Baruah, unlike Omvedt, views the Assam movement not as one of self-determination and his concept of sub-nationalism within the frame of multinational India "is not substantially different from Guha's notion of Little Nationalism" (p 676). Regarding his use of the western concept of a 'Plural society', he pleads guilty of leaving "room for some misunderstanding". "Nowhere have I implied", he assures us, "that the concept is an alternative to class analysis or to the notion of a multinational India, as Guha contends" (p 679). He also says categorically that "the predominance of Bengalis in the higher echelons of the bureaucracy are now part of history." I am thankful to him for this clarification.

SELF-DETERMINATION

Baruah's other point that a distinction must be made between "the nationalism of a big nation and that of a small nation" (Lenin) is a valid one. That is why not only the question of autonomy but also equality of all languages and nationalities, big and small, comes up. According to Lenin, proletarian internationalism must rest "not only in the observance of the formal equality of nations but even in an inequality of the oppressor nation, the great nation". He concluded his note by saying: "it is better to overdo the concessions and leniency towards the national minorities"[15].

This was Lenin's last advice on the national question, which he gave three weeks before his death in connection with the complicated Georgian case in 1922. P. Sundarayya's note, as quoted above in section I, shows how the left incorporated this point in their conceptualization of the national question in its northeast Indian context.

Even in the absence of an oppressor nation in India, Lenin's teaching is unmistakably there for us in the realm of relationships between the numerically big and small nationalities. If this is not kept in mind, then surely many of us having faith in socialism and democracy in the Hindi-speaking and Bengali-speaking areas - even though otherwise progressive - might become victims of big nationality chauvinism. But those from small nationalities also have lessons to draw upon. Lenin said in another context earlier in 1913: "A Social-Democrat from a small nation must emphasize in his agitation the second word of our general formula 'voluntary integration' of nations .... In all cases, he must fight against *small nation narrow-mindedness, seclusion and isolation, consider the whole and the general, subordinate in particular to the general interest* (emphasis added)[16]. It appears that Hiren Gohain's controversial articles, wherein he called the Assam agitation a cudgel of chauvinism, amongst other things, were written in a spirit of fighting this very trend as well as the other tendency to dominate over the tribal national groups.

Now, does the left's programme, as briefly sketched above in section I, go against Lenin's teachings in intent and deed? Is the left's concern for giving Nepali and Santali languages a special status in West Bengal or for the extension of a Sixth Schedule-type autonomy to Tripura tribal areas to preserve the Tripuri cultural identity, in the face of fierce Bengali chauvinism, a sign of their incorrect handling of the small nationality problem? Did not they consistently champion "the legitimate desire of the Assamese-speaking people to make their language the predominant factor in their life as the medium of education and administration" and the cause of linguistic state (Sundarayya)? Baruah thinks that the left had not done enough "to articulate the cultural demands of vulnerable nationalities", nor had it "adequately fought for the specific economic demands of these backward areas" such as Assam (p 681). To bring up the question of 'adequacy' is the easiest way of putting the blame on some scapegoat, since the gap between efforts and achievement could always be mechanically interpreted as the result of inadequate efforts. When skeptics indulge in such platitudes, it is difficult to provide an answer, particularly when they remain oblivious of the complex facts of life and see a problem not as a whole, but only in part.

The Asamiyas are not the only 'vulnerable' national group or the only 'basic' population in Assam, not even in the Brahmaputra Valley, which latter territory provides a common homeland also to the plains tribal population - the Bodos and the Mishings living in pockets of concentration. At a stage when the formation of the Assamese nationality is yet incomplete, one has to take into account not one but several sub-nationalisms that are at work and find ways to co-ordinate and balance their aspirations in a manner that would help the Assamese nationality formation as well as the Indian unity in view. Had this been kept in mind and had he examined the left's stand in specific details, Baruah would have been less harsh in his criticism of the left, notwithstanding their relative failures, and would not have provided an apologia for the outburst of chauvinism in Assam. It is somewhat puzzling to find that his understanding of the decades-old Asamiya movement has a reference neither to its attitudes to the plains tribal people's national aspirations nor to the problems of the formation of a greater Assamese nationality through voluntary integration of all such diverse national groups and elements.

'Big' and 'small', 'dominant' and 'non-dominant' - these are relative terms that attain their meanings in association with the context as well as the cases put forward for a comparison. The Bengalis and the Asamiyas - each constitutes a small, insignificant part of the Indian society at large, as compared to the Hindi-speakers. Both are dominated by non-Asamiya and non-Bengali big capital. Economic stagnation today is felt harder in Assam than in West Bengal, no doubt. But both have frustrations and feelings of insecurity peculiar to themselves; Assam, from the haunting burden of immigration; and West Bengal, also from the backlog of other partition-induced problems. But, when compared to each other, the Bengalis appear to be a 'big' and the Asamiyas a 'small' national group. Hence, in Baruah's order of priorities, the Assamese/Asamiya cause (its identity crisis, etc.) gets precedence over the Bengali settlers' cause in Assam. What is not clear from his articles is whether the same logic is to be extended also to the advantage of the other small national groups of Assam. For example, within the Assam State (in the Brahmaputra Valley in particular), the Asamiyas are a relatively 'big', and the Bodos a 'small' nationality. The plains tribal movement for a separate script and state (which is perhaps reducible to the demand for an autonomous area within the state) also stands for the restoration of all transferred lands to their original tribal peasant proprietors, in areas which, in 1948, were decided to be demarcated as reserved tribal blocs. If fully given effect to, such a measure would involve the ejectment of thousands of settlers - mostly the so-called foreigners and, to a much lesser extent, also Asamiyas. Under the circumstances, the national question in Assam will not be solved unless what is progressive and just in the tribal aspirations is also attended to. Any demonstration of big nationality chauvinism, whether it is of Asamiya origins or of Bengali origins, has to be denounced in no unequivocal terms. But nowhere in his survey of the Assam problem does Baruah mention this dimension, although the tribal little nationalists and sections of the CPI (ML) have already raised the bogey of Asamiya 'big' nationality chauvinism in relation to the tribals.

If large-scale deportation even after a gap of a generation is agreed upon in principle as a permissible measure to set at right past injustice, then it will not stop at driving out the so-called foreigners only, but will also reach out to the non-tribal Asamiya settlers in the submontane tribal blocs of the

Brahmaputra Valley. This complex situation, therefore, warrants a consideration of the whole, and the general, and a subordination of the particular to the general interest, while providing a solution. Baruah should have spelt out how and in what manner inadequacies in the left's stand could be plugged, in terms of such specific aspects.

Not that Baruah has not specified some of the plausible measures that could ameliorate the Assamese fear of a loss of identity. He suggests separation of Bengali-speaking Cachar district *(The Statesman,* December 13, 1980) from the state, "reorganization of Assam and constitutional measures for protecting the rights of Assam's basic population in future" *(EPW,* April 11, 1981), and other protective measures as are found useful in states with special status like Jammu and Kashmir, Nagaland and Meghalaya. The broad frame of the left's stand (Sundarayya's note) on the national question, as it appears to me, does not rule out any or all such measures.

But, given the sensitive circumstances, how could they, the left, "take the initiative in formulating a positive programme" in the matter of details, as demanded by Baruah, at this stage? Did not they burn their fingers once, while facing the Pakistan movement, then described by many as a Muslim nationality upsurge? (The frenzy amongst Bengali Muslims I saw then as a young student in 1946 was no different in spirit from what was seen in Assam amongst the Asamiya Hindus in 1979 and 1980). The demand for a 'yes' or 'no' reply on such proposals may metaphysically seem a practical one. But in practice it is not. The left has to subordinate such demands to the interests of the class struggle. You cannot say in advance whether any or all of these measures will help remove the 'fear' of the Asamiya people or, on the contrary, will be taken as an affront to their sensitivities regarding identity. That is why the left, at this stage, can point out only to the feasibility of such measures, and the risks of attaining these at the expense of another national group, particularly if it is small and non-dominant. It is not for the left to jump into the bandwagon of little nationalism in any form - be it the *Ujani Rajya Parishad* (separate Upper Assam State), *Udayachal Rajya* (separate state for Assam's plains tribals), Greater Bengal or the Deportation platform - to appease the concerned alien classes. Baruah's ideas are, however, most welcome as a feeler, and one must wait and see how the AASU-AAGSP forces and others react to these, when presented in more concrete and co-ordinated form by him at an opportune moment. All such ideas of Baruah fall within the purview of political reforms in the realm of Centre-State relations. In fact, one of the left, parties, SUCI, has already demanded a constitutional safeguard for continuation of Asamiya as the state language of Assam for all times to come, independently of the population composition.

THREAT TO IDENTITY: MYTH OR REALITY?

To suggest that I hold the view that "immigration poses no threat to cultural identity" (p. 677) is a crudity. What I tried to show is that immigration is not necessarily a threat, if there is assimilation as a counter-veiling force side by side. Immigration as well as the foreigner question was given due cognizance in my treatment in a historical perspective. My contention was that the chauvinists' presentation of the issues is full of exaggerations, myths and motivations other than mere identity preservation. I provided illustrations from the official thinking of the Asam Sahitya Sabha - a constituent of the AAGSP to show this. If there are clouds in the form of threats to identity, there is also a silver lining of hope in the form of the Asamiya society's capacity to Asamiyaise the immigrants over the years.

I also emphasized that what was just and progressive in little nationalism, including such demands as separation of Sylhet and restrictions on immigration, was incorporated into the Congress and left programme during pre-Independence decades. Nevertheless, a separate little nationalist platform was still in existence, by and large, as a tool of imperialism rather than of the national freedom movement, during 1920-1947. It was albeit mostly packed with Congress drop-outs, loyalists and client intellectuals. I also showed that Asamiya little nationalism became basically aggressive and chauvinistic after 1947, although such a change could not have sprouted overnight of nothing. In this connection, I showed that even Tarunram Phukan, an Indian nationalist by all means, gave vent to such feelings in an unbuttoned moment from the Asam Sahitya Sabha platform in 1927, a year marked by Asamiya-Bengali middle-class conflict over the apple of discord - Goalpara.

In contrast to his rationalization of Tarunram Phukan's stand, Baruah's treatment of Fakhruddin Ali Ahmed, another Assamese leader of all India stature, is too obviously shabby and intriguing. Ali Ahmed's father, Zalnur Ali Ahmed (1848-1931) came of a poor, indigenous Asamiya family of Kacharihat, near Golaghat town of Upper Assam. He rose to be a member of the Indian Medical Service and, while in service, married into an aristocratic Urdu-speaking family of Delhi. He made Delhi his second home. Fakhruddin Ali Ahmed was brought up outside Assam and, on graduation from Cambridge, came back to his paternal house at Guwahati around 1935 to practice law. Because of this background he could not reportedly speak his father's language fluently. But this did not come in the way of his serving Assam as a nationalist Muslim all through his life since then. He was elected President of India in recognition of his role in the freedom fight in Assam, his abilities and other usual considerations of a bourgeois party. *Baruah* introduces him as "Assam's best known *migrant* (?) leader" (p. 680, emphasis and question mark mine) and cites a non-Assamese reporter to ridicule his lack of fluency in Asamiya. Indeed this 'summarises the predicament of Assam's basic population" more meaningfully than Devakanta Barooah's reported attitude to the "Alis (immigrant Bengali Muslims) and the coolies (the garden workers)". That Bagh Hazarika, an Asamiyaised Muslim, was a right-hand man to the 17th century hero, Lachit Phukan, in the resistance to the Mughals, or the fact that the indigenous Assamese Muslims accounted for 9 per cent of the population of the Brahmaputra Valley as far back as in 1881, long before the influx, are often conveniently forgotten to deny their descendants the rights of a 'basic' population. From such attitude, it is but one step to a racial concept of a 'basic' population.

"From their second generation", I argued, "the Bengali migrants' major dialect, Mymensinghia, began to borrow words and even idioms from their Asamiya neighbours. As a result, by now, their dialect - like Sadri or Garden-baat spoken in the gardens and ex-tea garden villages - is increasingly gravitating to Asamiya". Baruah accepts the evolution of "neo-Assamese dialects such as Sadri" as "persuasive evidence on the trends towards assimilation" (p. 679), but avoid mentioning Mymensinghia (also known as Bhatiali) in this connection; perhaps, he has reservations to accept my contention fully, or even that of E.H. Parkentein, Superintendent of Assam Census, 1961, who noted that because of the distance of their dialect from standard Bengali, Muslim Bengalis immigrating into the Brahmaputra Bailey "have a tendency to return Assamese as their mother-tongue even in pre-independence days"[17], when the question of political motivation for this could not arise.

Baruah's reservations about the use of Census raw data are understandable. Limitations of such data are known, and could be largely overcome, to arrive at fair estimates, after cross-checking with other sources. One could introduce in analysis methodological sophistications, but in no case could the census series be discarded as totally useless. Enrolment registers of schools and colleges could also be examined to find out what number of neo-Asamiyas offer Asamiya as their first or school language as a matter of choice. One could even scan through the pages of the published Asamiya literature to see how the process of Asamiyaisation is reflected spontaneously in Asamiya periodicals and literature. Incidentally, one feature I noted during the current agitation is that the local minorities of the Brahmaputra Valley have tried to agitate against the movement mainly through the medium of Asamiya periodicals (e.g., *Nagarik and Mojahed).* It is these facts that convince me of the efficacy of the going assimilation process. However, further research and survey to clinch the issue are welcome.

Even allowing for wide margins of error, our statistical exercise throws some light on the problem and sets limits to exaggerations. Until convincing evidence, based on a more rigorous methodology, is produced to disprove my contention, there is no reason why I should subscribe to the other theory that the political-cultural identity of the Asamiya people is already seriously threatened and cannot be salvaged unless all the East Bengal immigrants of 1951-1971 period with no valid documents are physically deported. The foreigner problem could surely be solved in a more humane, non-racist and democratic way by stopping further influx, by encouraging assimilation of all pre-1971 settled immigrants of Indian origin and by those other suitable measures, as suggested by Baruah. I agree with Baruah when he says: "A solution of the crisis is admittedly difficult specially within the terms laid down by the agitators" *(The Statesman,* December 13, 1980, emphasis added).

THE CLASS AXIS AND LEFT STRATEGY

Baruah's discovery that I used the term, 'middle class/ classes', valiantly - sometimes in an 'expanded' sense to include 'upper classes or bourgeois landlord chauvinists' occupying the middle positions in the economy and sometimes in a narrower sense to mean the petty bourgeoisie only - is not correct. A scrutiny of his own citations from my October article will suffice to bear me out. The very first citation, for instance, reveals that my concept of a middle class, did include, *inter alia,* industrialists, traders and petty landlords. Again, according to his own admission, the concept I projected of the Asamiya middle class is also inclusive of 'small capitalists and professionals and service-holders many of whom are 'simultaneously small landlords'. Yet in another place of my article (p 1705), the Asamiya middle class (or classes) was said to be constituted of bourgeois, landlord and petty bourgeois elements. In fact my numerous references to the middle class/ classes invariably included bourgeois and landlord strata appropriate to the context. So, Baruah's discovery is somewhat embarrassing.

Baruah objects to my concept of the Asamiya middle class/classes, as a mobiliser of the people in the struggle for power. He thinks that, thereby, I misplaced the hegemonic role, historically belonging to a nascent bourgeois class, to a motley crowd (i.e. the crowd of petty bourgeoisie). In my analysis, 'middle class/classes' emerge as an amalgam of various strata of the bourgeoisie and petty bourgeoisie, and, in the given context, also petty landlords (gentry). This is not generally done by the Marxists. Surely, therefore, I owe an explanation to my readers, as Omvedt also pointed out.

The term, middle class, has no standard, rigid meaning in Marxist usage. It is now generally used to mean the petty bourgeoisie; but, sometimes, it also exclusively stands for a nascent bourgeoisie supposed to have the hegemonic role[18]. Hence, from a formal point of view, the terms, 'bourgeois' and 'middle class', could be used interchangeably, depending on the historical context. However, my lumping up of middle bourgeois, petty bourgeois and petty landlords (gentry) together and then using "middle class" as an omnibus term was an oversimplification, deliberately done to pinpoint their more or less equally important roles in the Assam movement, as its driving force. Nowhere did I use the term hegemony or 'hegemonic class' in my article, for that would have raised additional questions, not very relevant to our immediate context. In any case, hegemonic or not, classes do have their respective ideologies and notions of ways to power.

Despite some misunderstanding, Baruah is aware of my viewing regional nationalism as an ideology of the regional small capitalists and Indian nationalism as an ideology of the relevant big bourgeoisie. In both cases, I emphasise the bourgeois class content. I, also, showed how the Asamiya nascent bourgeois (whatever be their numerical strength) drew, gradually, the entire petty bourgeoisie into its fold. "The agitation was started by the Asamiya capitalists and gentry through the communication media they control, and the students and other sections of the petty bourgeoisie including sections of peasants were gradually drawn into it" (p. 1705). Had it been started by the students by themselves, the agitation would have still remained a bourgeois (or middle class) movement in essence by virtue of the logic of substitutism or because of its ideological roots in that class. Small capitalists in Assam - owners of tea gardens, leased-out paddy lands, small factories and printing presses - have many petty bourgeois and gentry characteristics, and they are in professions and top echelons of services as well. They surely constitute a nascent bourgeois class looking forward to autonomy and more power at the state level. These considerations prompted me to use the term "middle class", always in an expanded sense. I have also noted the duality of their two level national consciousness, regional and all-India with an overlap.

In my opinion, not only that the use of the term 'middle class/classes' in its restored classical sense is valid, but its use in an expanded sense is also permissible, if its purpose-specific definition is provided, for purposes of explaining the complex Indian situation. By middle classes I have generally meant both the bourgeoisie and the petty bourgeoisie in the context of the struggle against big bourgeois stranglehold over the economy.

Why, at all, at the initial stage of the agitation, did the local Marwari business houses fraternize with the agitators providing them with apples, oranges, money and petrol? Was it their paying a ransom? It is also a mystery as to how these houses and AAGSP local bosses, between them, turned the plywood blockade into a mockery in the long run, making some people conspicuously rich in that process. Whatever be the explanation of such queer phenomena, let me point out that I wrote about the cudgel of chauvinism helping the agitators "to win over to their cause or at *least neutralize"* (p. 1706, emphasise added) such houses, and not simply 'win over' as Baruah suggests. This, I think, meets his points.

Are top professionals such as thriving lawyers, doctors, professors and high-ranking government servants necessarily petty bourgeoisie? Mao-Tse-tung faced this problem when presenting a neat class analysis of the Chinese society. Amongst the various strata of the Chinese petty bourgeoisie listed therein are included lower government functionaries, *small* lawyers and primary and *secondary school* teachers, but not certainly the higher government functionaries, big lawyers and university teachers[10]. The latter are not mentioned even as constituents of the other classes- bourgeois and proletariat. It appears, therefore, that by implication, Mao placed them in one or the other category of the bourgeoisie or as their attached associates. Such are the complexities of class alignments in every country, in every situation, that defy a tight classification[20].

Hair-splitting logic and over-precision are the usual arts of the growing tribe of Marxiologists, not of the Marxists. For the latter approximations that help understand the complexities of a social reality and provide a guide to action are reasonably valid. It is for them to relate all social up-heavals and developments to the underlying class conflicts, hidden or open, however class-neutral these might appear in populist garb. Marxism ceases to be so when it views a social movement as amorphous and sees only crowds in action, not the class or classes behind it.

Baruah holds that "nationalist political interventions do not, in themselves, have a determinate class content", though "most nationality upsurges occur within the hegemony of bourgeois ideology" (p. 680). This position is not acceptable. All the rest of Baruah's arguments - that nationalities do not have rights in a vacuum, that in themselves the symbols of an eco-system (the raw materials for populist mobilization) are class-neutral, that politics and ideologies of nationalities have "relative autonomy" etc., etc. - are acceptable statements. But a nationality grows by way of assimilating diverse and mobile elements. The national rights belong to the expanded base, not to a particular racial group, and the assimilated groups get emotionally attached to the common eco-symbols in due course. Even in the relatively autonomous world of a superstructure, the class roots are not indeterminate. These could be traced back, just as the vanished Cheshire cat can be related to the grin hanging in the air. Nationalism is not class-neutral, although it may not maintain a one-to-one correlation with its economic base in time-space terms. In my analysis, I did trace the history of Asamiya nationalism and its anti-Bengali prejudices over the last hundred years and related this background to the current outburst of chauvinism (i.e., 'bellicose nationalism* according to the *Concise Oxford Dictionary).*

Two points may further be made. The persistent fear-psychosis, I said, "had an objective basis, too, during the British period", but this basis became "thin in the post-Independence period". This was so, I said, because of three reasons - (i) a reorganization of the state on the basis of linguistic considerations, (ii) the emergence of Asamiya as the official language of state administration and medium of University education and (iii) an expansion of its demographic base through assimilation of diverse elements. It is possible that census figures conceal more than what they reveal and that neo-Asamiyas, in sizeable numbers, might again shift their unstable language loyalties back to their original mother tongues. But no symptoms of such a *volt face en masse* were visible in Assam over the past few decades. On the contrary, many symptoms of increasing assimilation were, and are, in sight. In their third generation, many of the neo-Asamiyas cannot now be distinguished from the rest of the Asamiyas.

Deportation (made as painless as possible), says Baruah, "is perhaps indispensable today if the rights of the basic population have to be protected". Now, assuming that the Asamiya national existence is really precarious, how does deportation of a few lakh of people help preserve that existence? Will it not disrupt assimilation and thereby the very process of nationality formation? Will it not provoke linguistic reconversion of many more lakhs of the half-assimilated neo-Asamiyas and, thus, further complicate the situation? Besides, such an abominable persecution will lead to a counter-agitation and resistance, no less bellicose and immature than the AASU-AAGSP movement.

In fact, under the garb of various minority organizations, anti-left chauvinist elements are already active in the field, mouthing catchy slogans and using jingoist symbols the utility of which for mass mobilization was proved by their Asamiya counterparts. "If you are a true Asamiya, come out with your *hengdang"* (literally, short sword); and, "If we win our cause, we live above the soil; if we die for the cause, we rest below the *soil;* and if we are forced to go, we go with the *soil"*. Such were the slogans and counter-slogans that ominously stirred the people of the Brahmaputra Valley at the peak of the agitation and counter-agitation. Both sides exploited their attachment to the soil for rousing sentiments.

This is the real outcome of the so-called anti-foreigner movement. It refused to direct its thrust against the grip of foreign capital over Assam's plantation economy. It not only created a counter-productive environment of communal dissensions, mistrust and fear, but also an illusion amongst the minorities that without Delhi's benign authoritarian regime in the form of President's rule or a puppet ministry, their basic democratic rights would not be safe. Caught between the horns of a dilemma, the left's position, is nowhere else in India so unenviable as in Assam today. This situation demands that, while recognizing the historical legitimacy of Assam's populist nationality upsurge (however immature and chauvinist it may be), this recognition be strictly limited to what is progressive therein and be prevented from being 'an apologia for nationalism', a bourgeois ideology. In no case should it be allowed to obscure proletarian consciousness.

India's is not a plural but a mixed multinational society in which ethnic factors are in a melting pot. Here the solution of the problems of economic emancipation and autonomy lies essentially not in promoting further exclusivism and isolation, not in driving out settled toilers from one area to another (even if they are of foreign origins), but in uniting the national contingents of the toiling people against the wrong policies of the ruling classes. It would be a downright betrayal of democratic principles and a silly policy even from the standpoint of the Asamiya bourgeois's 'national aims' - if we are to abide by Leninist norms - to weaken the ties between the Asamiya and non-Asamiya toilers that now exist within the confines of a single state. No further influx across the frontiers and a 'National Policy' of encouraging assimilation - these are the only practical measures that could be accepted immediately without reservations to remove the fear of Assam's basic population. The status quo in terms of demographic balance, is not really as disturbing as it is often projected to be.

III

Finally, since the fear of losing identity, however irrational and obsolete now, survives in the Asamiya/Assamese psyche and since this fear complex is nevertheless a part of the present reality, Hiren Gohain's second thoughts *(EPW,* February 28) and Sanat Bose's loud thinking *(ibid,* April 4) deserve serious attention. Both the AASU-AAGSP forces and the political parties, now no more said to be irrelevant, must meet for finding out the basis for a just and democratic settlement of the foreigner problem, in its essence, on a give-and-take basis.

If there is agreement on speedy ejectment within limits of practicability of all *illegal* encroachers from forest lands, railway lands and reserved tribal blocs, irrespective of caste, creed and community considerations, with due provision for compensation and resettlement and through a specially constituted national Commission, then given the prospects of assimilation, 90 per cent of the hurdles will vanish. For, the problem would then be reduced to the ordinary problem of vacating encroachments. In other words, persons proved to be encroachers could be ejected and resettled in the same manner in which Bengali refugee settlers in reserved tribal areas of Tripura or squatters in the Marichjhahpi area of West Bengal were dealt with. As to stopping further influx from Bangladesh and Nepal, with retrospective effect from 1971 and 1976 respectively, there is already a national policy that emerged under the pressure of the agitation. This is a major gain not to be thrown away. The status of Asamiya language in administration and universities is well entrenched. Further, *the agitators willing,* Bose's and Baruah's other proposals like a constitutional provision providing safeguards for continuation of the existing state-level official languages, a vivisection of the state of Assam to separate the Bengali-speaking Cachar district, an extended use of the Sixth Schedule, as and when found convenient, to maximize the autonomy of claimant national groups.

However, in the situation of a clash between 'nationalism' and humanism, between toilers' unity and parochialism, the left should know which side of the barricade they belong to. They need not be shy of calling Assam's current little nationalist agitation immature, chauvinist and often parochial even while upholding what is just in it and taking note of its capacity to misguide the masses.

One should not also, even for a moment, forget that the national question today is a special area of operation for the neocolonialist policy-makers. US imperialists now come out as super champions of 'self-determination' and they provide motivated research, readymade blue-prints, know-how and patronage to all varieties of nationalism with a view to blunting proletarian consciousness in general and destabilizing States *non grata* in particular[21]. There are reasons to suspect that the lingering of the Assam agitation, despite positive response to the kernel of its demands, and its leaders' sole emphasis on an impracticable cut-off year for foreigner's identification to the neglect of all other positive developmental demands, stem from the influence Rotarians and Lions and trade unionists-turned-planters' advisers exert from within it. The Assam agitation surely developed out of the internal contradictions of the Indian society, but also under external conditions of neo-colonialist interest and interventions that oil-rich northeast India attracts. A speedy solution of the problem is, therefore, all the more urgent under the circumstances, so that such elements get .isolated from the concerned patriotic masses and a positive movement for economic development, self-reliance and real autonomy of the

Assamese people could be launched unitedly by the state's left and democratic forces.

REFERENCES

1. *Pamuar Sont Bandh Karibalai aru Agantuk Grihakandalarpara Asamak Raksha Karibalai Comiunist Partir Ahvan* (in Asamiya), Guwahati, n d, pp. 4-5.
2. Assam, Provincial, Organising Committee, CPI, Assam *Fights for Freedom and Democracy:* Draft Resolutions of Assam Communists Guwahati, n d, pp. 41-50,
3. Assam Government in the Dock, Guwahati, 1967, p. 7.
4. CPI (M), Work Report (Political) of the Central Committee to the Ninth Congress, Organisational Position of the Party (Tables). Note on National Question and Amendment to Party Programme Adopted by the Ninth Congress Calcutta, 1972, p. 94.
5. Collection of Resolutions and Statements of Assam State Committee, CPI (M), *Bideshi Nagarikar Samasya Samparkat Marksvadi Communist Partir Baktavya* (in Asamiya, Guwahati, March 1980), pp 3-11 (on p. 3, read 1978 for '70).
6. *The Assam Tribune,* November 8,1979
7. Collection of Resolution, n 5, pp. 27-30; translation mine.
8. *ibid.*
9. *ibid.*
10. *Bharatar Comunist Partir Asam Pradeshik Sanmilan: Rajnaitik Prastay: Pratham Adhiveskan,* Guwahati, February 1948, pp. 16-17.
11. 'Note on the national question and amendment to party pro-gramme' in CPI (M), *Work Report...* n 4, pp. 95-108.
12. *People's Democratic Party, Assam: Draft Programme and Constitution* (in Asamiya), Guwahati, n d.
13. P. Sundarayya, *National Integration: A Critique of Government Policies,* Calcutta, 1974, pp. 20-23.
14. For the quotes, *ibid,* pp. 23 and 25.
15. V.I. Lenin, *Collected Works,* Vol 36, Moscow, 1966, pp. 608-9.
16. *ibid*, Vol 22, p. 347.
17. Cited by Birendrakumar Bhattacharyya, "Language Controversy in Assam: Socio-Economic Background and the Need for a

National Policy" *North Eastern Research Bulletin* (Dibrugarh), Vol. 4, September 1973, p. 11.

18. For example, the following passage in *Revolution and Counter Revolution in Germany:* "The political movement of the middle class, or bourgeoisie in Germany, may be dated from 1840. It had been preceded by symptoms showing that the moneyed and industrial class of that country was ripening, into a state which would no longer allow it to continue apathetic and passive under the pressure of a half-feudal, half-bureaucratic monarchism". *See Collected Works, Vol. 11, Marx and Engels 1851-1853,* Moscow, 1979, p. 13. Many such instances could be given from other writings of Marx and Engels.
19. "Analysis of the classes in Chinese society" in *Selected Works of Mao-Tse-Tung,* Vol. I, Calcutta, 1972, pp. 13-19.
20. As to the petty bourgeois character of the Assamese bourgeois class and its potentialities or the use of "bourgeois' and 'middle class' as interchangeable terms. I had somewhat a different view, in 1974, that was closer to Baruah's rather than to my current position. See, Hiren Gohain's "Origins of the Assamese Middle class", *Social Scientist,* August 1973 and my comment *ibid,* January-February 1974. For further information on and an analysis of the Asamiya middle class, see my paper "Assamese Agrarian Society in the Late Nineteenth Century: Roots, Structures and Trends" *Indian Economy and Social History Review,* Vol 17, November 1, January-March, 1980.
21. J.E. Jackson's address to the 22nd National Convention of the CPUSA in August 1979, *Political Affairs,* February 1980. The connection between US funding organizations - some of them CIA-linked - and social science research on the weak links of developing societies is well-known.

Letters to Editor

Assamese People's Agitation*

Most of the articles appearing in Left journals have been hostile to the Assamese peoples' agitation, perhaps with reason, given the undoubted brutality shown against Bengali-speakers and the active role of many reactionary forces.

But I am still not convinced. There are some fundamental questions - fundamental from the view of a communist response, not journalistic exposure - that have not been dealt with thoroughly by the writers.

(1) Is the Assamese peoples' agitation fundamentally one of chauvinism or of national self-determination? This is not a question of the progressive - or - reactionary nature of the leadership but of the fundamental class/ national characteristics of the society and the movement. I am puzzled as to how in particular those Marxists who characterize India as a 'multinational' country can so lightly throw around the concept of 'chauvinism'?

(2) If the movement is fundamentally around issues of national self-determination, should the response of communists be to condemn it because the leadership is reactionary or to take part and attempt to provide an alternative leadership?

---

* *EPW,* Vol. XV, No. 12, March 22,1980, p. 580.

(3) Is there any objective basis for the fear of the Assamese people that they and their cultural-national identity may be swept by the Bengali influx? If there is, then what kind of assurance that this won't happen has been given - historically and at present - by the communities?

(4) Is the CPI (M) really based only among the Bengalis in Assam? If this is true after 50 years of communist presence in the area, then isn't it understandable that the Assamese people find it hard to understand what communism means?

GAIL OMVEDT
Kasegaon
March, 11

Little Nationalism Turned Chauvinist*

I have just read Amalendu Guha's article on Assam in your-Special Number, October 1980. Although I am in sympathy with most of his main conclusions, I feel he is unduly biased in favour of the CPI (M) as far as his reporting on the resistance to chauvinism is concerned.

It is quite absurd of him to claim that Uttam Barthakur, the Marxist student leader, is a CPI (M) cadre who infiltrated AASU in order to thwart chauvinist trends. Amalendu Guha ought to have known that the CPI (M) leadership has carried on a continuous campaign of slander and denunciation against the CPI (M-L) precisely for attempting such a manner of dealing with AASU. Uttam Barthakur's very election to the general secretaryship of the union society at Cotton College, the premier college in Assam, was achieved due to the direct support of the United Students' Federation (USF), the student organisation which is close to tie orientation of the CPI (M-L). For Amalendu Guha's information I would like to put on record the fact that AASU leaders such as Brojen Mahanta and Hareswar Burman, long members of the CPI (M-L), have tried since 1972 to

* *EPW*, Vol. XV, No. 4, January 24,1981, p. 91.

democratize AASU and indeed had achieved majority in the executive by 1977-78. It was in the next year that the Assamese bourgeois-landlord clique went flat out to turn AASU back into their own instrument and captured the executive by un-democratic methods. At that point, thousands of AASU activists, under the leadership of Uttam Barthakur and others, joined the USF en masse. The CPI (M) and its student wing, the SFI, had nothing to do with this process except to supply the leaven of their usual slanders.

Amalendu Guha's article does not mention the CPI (M-L) even once. Does he not know of the nearly 30,000 strong demonstration against chauvinism in Guwahati by the CPI (M-L) in September 1978? Even the chauvinist press in Assam reported it on their front pages. Or of the hundreds of CPI (M-L) activists arrested by sections of the chauvinist police? Or of the three score or so CPI (M-L) cadres seriously injured by chauvinist violence? Or, indeed, of the two CPI (M-L) comrades killed by the chauvinists? Instead he has discovered CPI martyrs when even the CPI has not claimed any such martyrdom. For this last error he may, at least, blame what I believe to be a misprint in the PUCL, Delhi, report, but what about the commissions?

Amalendu Guha even cites an article by K.M. Sharma in your journal, but does he know that Sharma is a well-known militant who officiates as a CPI (M-L) district secretary? It is amazing that so old an Assam hand as Amalendu Guha should be so conspicuously in the dark about an important aspect of the anti-chauvinist movement.

ARUNROY
Secretary, North Bengal Regional Committee,
CPI (M-L), Jalpaiguri,
January 17

Little Nationalism Turned Chauvinist*

I am grateful indeed to Arun Roy for his informative letter (January 24). He points out that Uttam Barthakur is associated not with the CPI (M) as stated incorrectly in my article (Special Number, October 1980). This error of fact as well as my failure to mention the CPI (M-L) "even once" as an important mobiliser of the forces of anti-chauvinism in Assam - both stem from typing mistakes (dropping of 'L' after 'CPI-M' in two places) that had crept into my typescript and had remained there due to an oversight. Incidentally, I also find that in one place in my article, the word 'phoenix-like' has become 'sphynx-like'. There is indeed many a slip between the pen and the printing press!

Let me clarify that not only the CPI (M), but also the CPI, RCPI, SUCI, CPI (M-L) and RSPI have taken a principled stand against the chauvinist agitation in Assam. All of them have, more or less, been the targets of its violence, just as other political parties and individuals, opposed to chauvinism, have been. I do not claim to have given (or the competence to give) a consolidated and complete list of all those who had laid down their lives while resisting chauvinism in Assam. In fact, not two - as I had earlier stated - but three CPI (M) cadres became

* *EPW, Vol.* XVI, No. 7, February 14,1981, p. 218.

martyrs to the cause. And now I learn from Arun Roy that two CPI (M-L) cadres also were killed by the chauvinists. All these facts establish the general anti-left character of the agitation and falsify the theory that, among the left parties, the CPI (M) alone stood isolated from the misguided patriotic Asamiya masses because its own 'follies' on the 'foreigner' question.

Arun Roy's frivolous charge that I have "discovered CPI martyrs when even the CPI has not claimed any such martyrdom" is unjustified and irresponsible. That five CPI cadres (members and sympathizers) lost their lives, while under attack from the chauvinists, was reported in the CPI's central organ, New Age, June 8, 1980, and also in Dadhi Mahanta's editorial article in the organ of the CPI's Assam State Committee, *Janamat,* May 26,1980. These sources give those martyrs' names as follows: Bihuram Boro and Habiran Boro of North Gauhati, Amulya Pandit and Rama Baishya of Nalbari and Prabhas Acharya of Sapekhati. So, it is not correct to say that "CPI has not claimed any such martyrdom".

At this critical juncture in Assam even basic human rights like the freedom of expression are daily coming under attack from both the chauvinist agitator and bureaucratic authoritarianism. It is, therefore, high time that the left parties bury their petty quarrels and work together for creating an alternative united platform which is capable not only of defeating chauvinism but also, at the same time of removing the patriotic Assamese masses' fear of being outnumbered and culturally absorbed by outside. Apart from closing the Bangladesh-Assam border, some concrete measures in terms of constitutional and legal measures also have to be spelt out at this hour by the left, so that these could help remove the fear psychosis, even if it has no objective basis. Chauvinism can be defeated in the long run only through persistent ideological and political work, and not by invoking repression by organs of state power from above.

AMALENDUGUHA
Calcutta
February 6

Little Nationalism Turned Chauvinist*

Amalendu Guha's long article on the current Assam movement (Special Number, October 1980) is indeed informative and illuminating. His detailed analysis of the genesis of the present movement indicates his thorough acquaintance with the subject.

Having very little knowledge of the realities of the Assam problem, I dare not venture to write a critique of Guha's article. I cannot however help noting that it unfortunately contributes little towards a resolution of the problem and the establishment of the much desired "national peace". And yet, this in my opinion, is the most burning issue of the day.

That the Asamiya people are genuinely seized by a fear of losing their cultural identity in their own homeland as a result of influx of migrants from foreign countries (Bangladesh and Nepal) is an observed fact that can be hardly controverted. Whether this fear psychosis is based on objective facts or otherwise, there should not be any doubt that such fear is there as an element of the current objective situation.

Hence the immediate issue, before us all (irrespective of caste or community) is how to remove this fear through suitable

---

* *EPW,* Vol. XVI, No. 14, April 4,1981, pp. 599-600.

measures (and not pious sermons only) - economic, cultural and political, consistent with the overall needs, demands and progress of the nation at large.

The recent trend of events indicates that the problem cannot be solved unilaterally by the leaders of the Assam movement alone, in spite of their unique mass popularity, I feel a time has come when the AASU and AAGSP leaders should seriously try to self-critically review their political stand vis-a-vis their demands against the backdrop of their own political experience (of leading a mass struggle). Such a critical assessment will help them see whether

(1) all their demands are democratically just and immediately realizable;

(2) the Asamiya people's genuine grievances can be dispelled only by the act of physical deportation of all those whom the leaders of the movement consider foreigners on the basis of their own unilateral definition of foreigners; and

(3) the different all-India progressive political parties have become irrelevant from the point of view of this movement and hence there is no necessity of trying to involve these parties in this movement, through discussions and dialogues with a view to organising a common political platform and launching a powerful united democratic movement to force the powers that be to concede the Asamiya people's just demands.

I feel that if the leaders of the movement look beyond their present horizon in a-realistic way then they will be in a position to suggest alternatives, without compromising the genuine demands of the Asamiya people. For instance, something like (this is merely thinking aloud) a constitutional provision providing safeguards for continuation of the existing state-level official languages, separation of Cachar from Assam, speedy ejectment of all illegal encroachments on forest lands, railway properties, reserved tribal blocs (irrespective of caster or creed), through a specially constituted Commission with due provisions for compensation and rehabilitation, could be considered as some of the measures that would go a long way in overcoming the present fear psychosis.

So far the question of identifying and deporting foreigners is concerned, it seems that there cannot be any immediate drastic solution which can be implemented at once. The very nature of this complex problem indicates that serious collective discussions on the part of all well-wishers of the Asamiya people have to be arranged before some fruitful consensus emerges. This is the only realistic way of solving the problem.

Conversely, by sticking rigidly to their present stand, the AASU and the AAGSP may face the danger of getting more and more isolated from the general stream of democratic movements taking place all over the country. This in its turn may create a favourable situation for the ruling classes to actively intervene with a view to crushing the genuine aspirations of the Asamiya peoples by all sorts of repressive measures. In fact, there are enough indications of such a possibility, and if this policy of the reactionary ruling classes succeeds, it will not be confined in future to Assam alone. It will have far-reaching impact on all democratic movements throughout the country. Those who put their faith on state repressive actions for solving the Assam problem should be aware of this danger. As a matter of fact, the Assam issue is a direct challenge to all defenders of peace and democracy. Playing majority against minority communities and vice versa, has always been a typical tactic of the reactionary ruling classes for curbing peoples' democratic movements. The AASU and AAGSP leaders should therefore try to sort out their demands and rearrange them so that they may get active and direct support from all supporters and defenders of peace and democracy in the country.

SANTA BOSE
Calcutta
February 5

Little Nationalism Turned Chauvinist*

Sanjib Baruah (April 11) duly wins our admiration for his full-throated raptures at his own discoveries, but I see no reason to accept his qualification of my self-criticism as only 'half-hearted'. Since the point however is neither trivial nor personal, I feel bound to correct him here.

Actually my reservations about the CPI (M)'s views on the national question in Assam are a decade old and are derived from observations made from a modest amount of social practice. Let me quote from my review of Amalendu Guha's book, *Planter Raj to Swaraj,* published in *EPW* on April 1, 1978.

> Thus his treatment necessarily fails to throw any light on the exact relationship between the regions' bourgeoisie and the national big bourgeoisie. Guha also fails to be sufficiently critical of the class-character of the Congress leadership on the national scale. Hence, while he makes much of the chauvinist tendencies in the Assamese middle class, he is unable to see that this can be connected with the failure of the all-India leadership to solve the national question with wisdom and foresight. The tendency to dominate and browbeat the aspirations of small national groups was there among a considerable section of the national leadership from the very beginning. Guha

---

* *EPW,* Vol. XVI, No. 20, May 16, 1981, pp. 924.

> does not draw relevant conclusions from the data supplied by himself .... For instance, on many occasions the Assam leadership failed to agree with the views of the national leadership. . . . This may be of course considered in terms of the vested interests of the provincial leaders. But a more pertinent point is the inability of the national leadership to appreciate the difficulties of a neglected, backward and weak national group. . . . Against such a backdrop, the fears and worries of the Assamese are understandable. Seen in this light the conflict between little nationalism' and great nationalism . . . appears as a portentous failure of the bourgeois-democratic revolution in India.

Pretty strongly worded and quite categorical, I think! I am sorry Baruah whom I had in an earlier article told of this review, should find such statements less bold than his.

In 1969 I joined issue with the veteran CPI (M) leader, and Secretary of the Assam unit of the Party, Achintya Bhattacharyya publicly, and the article appeared in a collection *Sahitya Satya* in 1970. There I ventured to expound, very much like tilting against windmills, my reasons for disagreeing with the official CPI (M) line. In 1973 and 1974,1 again clashed with Amalendu Guha for his attempt to lump the Assamese regional bourgeoisie with the general petty-bourgeois masses of India, a position that had plenty of economic sense, but failed to explain the nature and thrust of Assamese nationalism. (See *Social Scientist,* August, 1973 and the discussion in the issue No. 18). It is important to mention these facts because at that time I was honestly trying to form a correct picture of Assamese society under the guidance of those veteran workers and scholars.

However, if I believe that they have failed to discern an important aspect of Assamese society and history, I do not think they have much to learn from Baruah. Baruah is so intoxicated with this image of a mass movement that he forgets it is natural for such a mass movement to develop and reveal all kinds of tendencies, some of which may indeed be revolutionary. But the main thrust and character of such movements depend on its more stable features, on its actual programme and its class-leadership. Looked at from this point of view the current movement in Assam definitely serves the interest of the Assamese small bourgeoisie and landlords, and is most likely to profit the big bourgeoisie. Consider the question of its position vis-a-vis the left. The strong and stable anti-communist orientation of the leadership, their tirades against the left, in season and out of season, the brutal selective murder of the communist cadres in the countryside, the atmosphere of terror and violence the leftists and democrats have to live under, give the lie to the blatant assertion that such things are only accidental 'excesses'. It is a fallacy to think that atrocities are some kind of divine punishment visited upon the left for a theoretical error, for these are plainly a use of mass-sentiment to destroy the left in a planned manner, by certain interested quarters. Yes, chauvinism is rather the henchman of the big bourgeoisie than the enemies of the left, I have a notion that the Assamese middle-class has failed to remain the national class it was up to the 50s.

People like Baruah could do well to submit to some self-criticism themselves, for their failure to see that in Marxism the concept of nationality is inevitably dialectical and that it degenerates the moment it loses its links with revolutionary internationalism. It is not of much help to parrot what Lenin had said on certain occasions, for in a different context he had made a different remark. A concrete, class-based analysis of the national question in India is badly needed.

HIREN GOHAIN
Nizarapar
Guwahati-6

APPENDIX

ASSAM ACCORD 15 AUGUST, 1985

Accord between AASU, AAGSP and Central Government, on the Foreign National issue

MEMORANDUM OF SETTLEMENT

1. Government have all along being most anxious to find a satisfactory solution to the problem of foreigners in Assam. The All Assam Student Union (AASU) and the All Assam Gana Sangram Parishad (AAGSP) have also expressed their keenness to find such a solution.
2. The AASU through their Memorandum dated 2nd February 1980 presented to the late Prime Minister Smt. Indira Gandhi, conveyed their profound sense of apprehensions regarding the continuing influx of foreign nationals into Assam and the fear about adverse effects upon the political, social, cultural and economic life of the State.
3. Being fully alive to the genuine apprehensions of the people of Assam, the then Prime Minister initiated the dialogue with the ASSU/AAGSP. Subsequently, talks were held at the Prime Minister's and Home Minister's levels during the period 1980-83. Several rounds of informal talks were held during 1984. Formal discussions were resumed in March, 1985.
4. Keeping all aspects of the problem including constitutional and legal provisions, international agreements, national commitments and humanitarian considerations, it has been decided to proceed as follows:-

Foreigners Issue

5.1 For purposes of detection and deletion of foreigners, 1.1.1966 shall be the base date and year.

5.2 All persons who came to Assam prior to 1.1.1966, including those amongst them whose names appeared on the electoral rolls used in 1967 elections, shall be regularized.

5.3 Foreigners who came to Assam after 1.1.1966 (inclusive) and up to 24th March 1971 shall be detected in accordance with the provisions of the Foreigners Act, 1946 and the Foreigners (Tribunals) Order 1964.

5.4 Names of foreigners so detected will be deleted from the electoral rolls in force. Such persons will be required to register themselves before the Registration Officers of the respective districts in accordance with the provisions of the Registration of Foreigners Act, 1939 and the Registration of Foreigners Rules, 1939.

5.5 For this purpose, the Govt. of India will undertake suitable strengthening of the government machinery.

5.6 On the expiry of a period of ten year following the date of detection, the names of all such persons which have been deleted from the electoral rolls shall be restored.

5.7 All persons who were expelled earlier, but have since re-entered illegally into Assam, shall be expelled.

5.8 Foreigners who came to Assam on or after March 25, 1971 shall continue to be detected, deleted and expelled in accordance with law. Immediate and practical steps shall be taken to expel such foreigner.

5.9 The government will give one consideration to certain difficulties expressed by the AASU/AAGSP regarding the implementation of the illegal migrants (Determination by Tribunals Act, 1983).

Safeguards and Economic Development

6. Constitutional, legislative and administrative safeguards, as may be appropriate, shall be provided to protect, preserve and

promote the cultural, social, linguistic identity and heritage of the Assamese people.

7. The government take this opportunity to renew their commitment for the speedy all round economic development of Assam, so as to improve the standard of living of the people. Special emphasis will be placed on education and science & technology through establishment of national institutions.

Other Issues

8.1 The government will arrange for the issue of citizenship certificates in future only by the authorities of the Central Government.

8.2 Specific complaints that may be made by the AASU/AAGSP about irregular issuance of Indian Citizenship Certificates (ICC) will be looked into.

9.1 The international border will be made secure against future infiltration by erection of barriers like walls, barbed wire fencing and other obstacles at appropriate places. Patrolling by security forces on land and riverine routes all along the international border shall be adequately intensified. In order to further strengthen the security arrangements, to prevent effectively future infiltration, an adequate number of check posts shall be set up.

9.2 Besides the arrangement mentioned above and keeping in view security considerations, a road all along the international border shall be constructed so as to facilitate patrolling by security forces. Land between border and the road shall be kept free of habitation, wherever possible. Riverine patrolling along the international border would be intensified. All effective measures would be adopted to prevent infiltrators crossing or attempting to cross the international border.

10. It will be ensured that relevant laws for prevention of encroachment of government lands and lands in tribal

belts and blocks are strictly enforced and unauthorized encroachers evicted as laid down under such laws.

11. It will be ensured that the relevant law restricting acquisition of immovable property by foreigners in Assam is strictly enforced.
12. It will be ensured that Birth and Death Registers are duly maintained.

Restoration of Normalcy

13. The All Assam Students' Union (AASU) and the All Assam Gana Sangram Parishad (AAGSP) call off the agitation, assure full co-operation and dedicate themselves towards the development of the country.
14. The Central and the State Government have agreed to:
    (a) review with sympathy and withdraw cases of disciplinary action taken against employees in the context of the agitation and to ensure that there is no victimization;
    (b) frame a scheme for ex-gratia payment to the next of kin of those who were killed in the course of the agitation;
    (c) give sympathetic consideration to proposal for relaxation of upper age limit for employment in public services in Assam, having regard to exceptional situation that prevailed in holding of academic and competitive examinations, etc. in the context of agitation in Assam;
    (d) undertake review of detention cases, if any, as well as cases against persons charged with criminal offences in connection with the agitation, except those charged with commission of heinous offences;
    (e) consider withdrawal of the prohibitory orders/ notifications in force if any.
15. The Ministry of Home Affairs will be the nodal Ministry for the implementation of the above.

Sd/-
(P.K. Mahanta)
President
All Assam Students' Union

Sd/-
(B.K. Phukan)
General Secretary
All Assam Students' Union

Sd/-
(R.D. Pradhan)
Home Secretary
Govt. of India

Sd/-
(Smt. P.P. Trivedi)
Chief Secretary
Govt. of Assam

Sd/-
(Biraj Sharma)
Convenor
All Assam Gana Sangram Parishad

In the presence of
Sd/-
(RAJIV GANDHI)
PRIME MINISTER OF INDIA

Date: 15th August, 1985.
Place: New Delhi.

1. Election Commission will be requested to ensure preparation of fair electoral rolls.
2. Time for submission of claim and objections will be extended by 30 days, subject to this being consistent with the Election Rules.
3. The Election Commission will be requested to send Central Observers.

Sd / - Illegible
HOME SECRETARY

1. Oil refinery will be established in Assam.
2. Central Government will render full assistance to the State Government in their efforts to re-open:
   (i) Ashok Paper Mill
   (ii) Jute Mills
3. I.I.T. will be set up in Assam.

Sd / - Illegible
HOME SECRETARY

❑❑❑

Index

B

C

❑❑❑